People AND Places

Silver Burdett Ginn
Parsippany, NJ • Needham, MA
Atlanta, GA   Deerfield, IL   Irving, TX   Santa Clara, CA

PROGRAM AUTHOR

Becky Manfredini
Early Childhood Consultant
Executive Director, KIDS AT HEART
Los Angeles, CA

 Silver Burdett Ginn
A Division of Simon & Schuster
299 Jefferson Road, P.O. Box 480
Parsippany, NJ 07054-0480

CONTENTS

iv

Maps

Map Adventures

Atlas Maps

Tables, Charts, and Diagrams

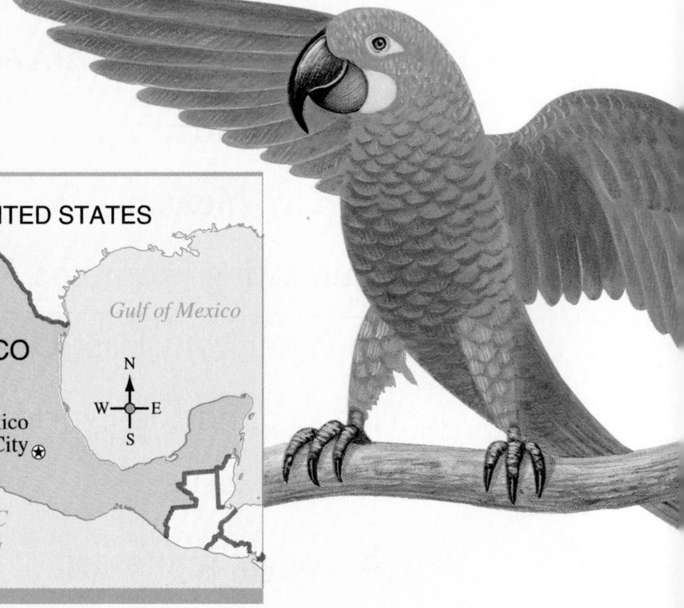

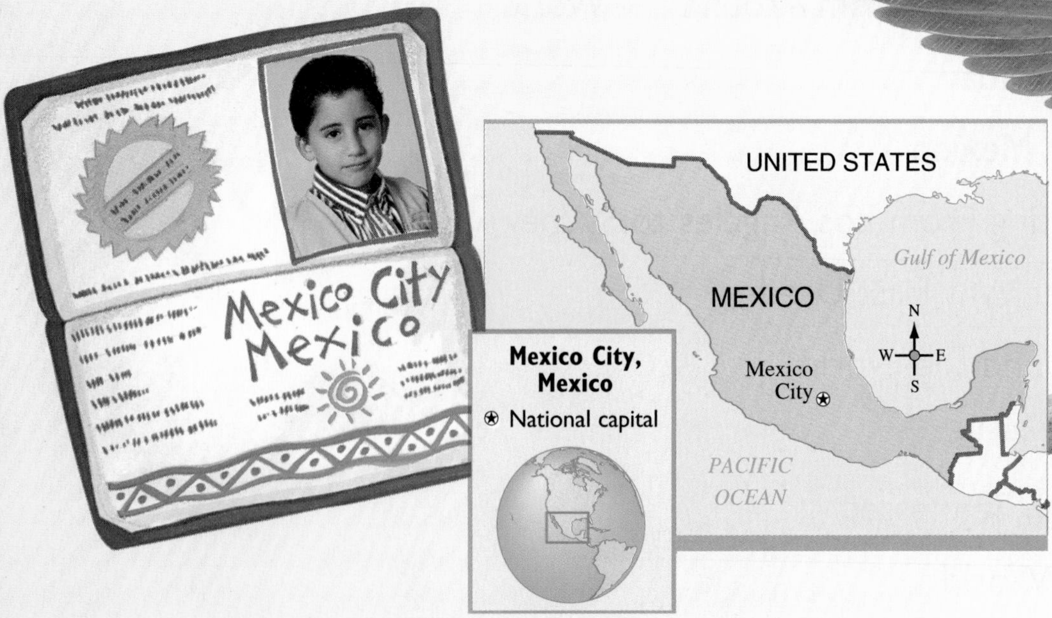

Mexico City
Mexico
UNITED STATES
Gulf of Mexico
MEXICO
N
W
E
S
Mexico City
PACIFIC OCEAN
Mexico City, Mexico
National capital

Literature

The following books are recommended for optional reading.

* available with Silver Burdett Ginn Social Studies

Map Handbook
CONTENTS

M8

Looking at

FLOOR PLANS

M10

How to **READ a MAP**

M12

Learning About **CONTINENTS**
and **OCEANS**

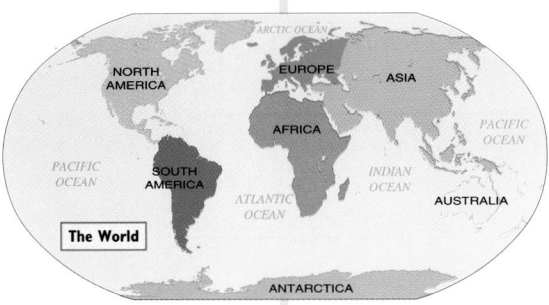

M14

Bodies of **WATER,**
Kinds of **LAND**

How to Use a
MAP KEY

Maps use small pictures or drawings to stand for real things. These pictures are called **symbols**. Map symbols often look like the things they stand for. For example, a drawing of a tent may be used to stand for a campground. The **map key** explains what each symbol stands for. It is usually in a box on the map.

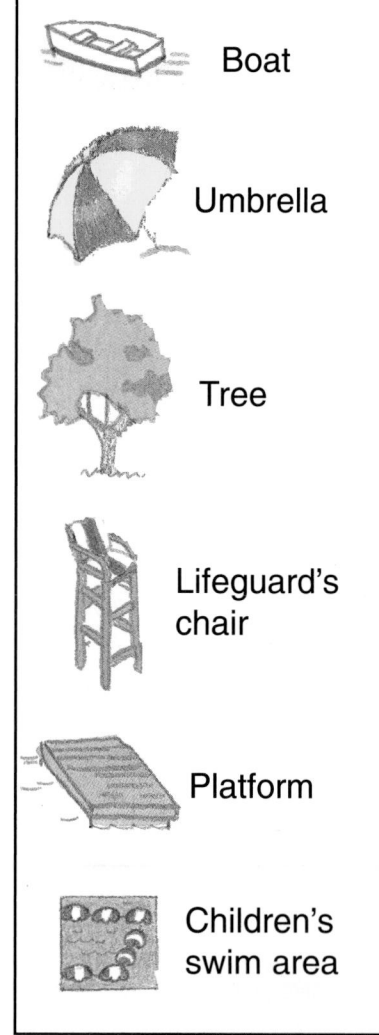

Boat

Umbrella

Tree

Lifeguard's chair

Platform

Children's swim area

Where's the Lifeguard?

- **Find the symbol for a lifeguard's chair in the map key.**
- **Now point to a lifeguard's chair on the map.**

Shady Spots

- **Use the map key. Find two places on the map where you could sit in the shade.**

Row, Row, Row Your Boat

- **Find the symbol for a boat in the map key.**
- **How many boats are on the map?**

Safety First

♦ Where should children swim? Use the map key to find the right place. Point to it on the map.

Now Try This!

Think about one of your favorite outdoor places. What things do you see there?
♦ Draw symbols for three of these things.
♦ Make a map key. Show your symbols and tell what they stand for.

How a MAP Is Like a PHOTOGRAPH

The photograph below was taken from an airplane. It shows a neighborhood. The map on page M5 shows the same neighborhood. Both the photograph and the map show a bird's-eye view. They show the neighborhood the way a bird flying overhead would see it.

The Same Shape

- Trace the shape of the ball field in the photograph with your finger.
- The key on a map tells the meaning of each color or symbol. Use the key to find the ball field on the map. Is it the same shape as the ball field in the photograph?

The Same Color

Things you see in the photograph sometimes have the same color on the map.

- How many swimming pools are on the map?
- Now find the pools in the photograph.
- Why do you think blue is used on the map to show the swimming pools?

Easy Does It!

- Trace the streets on the map with your finger.
- Now trace the streets in the photograph. Which way is easier?

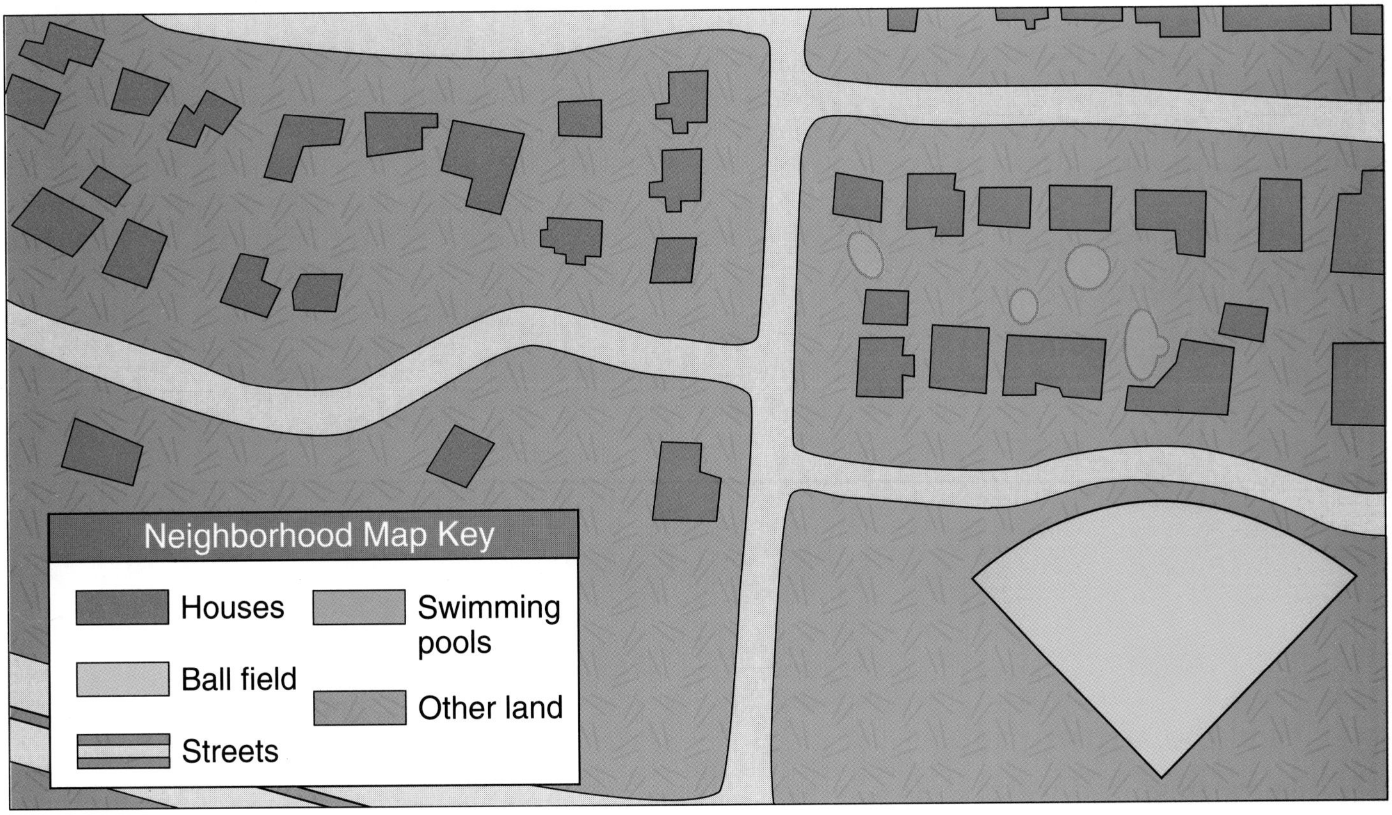

Neighborhood Map Key

- Houses
- Swimming pools
- Ball field
- Other land
- Streets

Now Try This!

Draw a map of your bedroom. Show the things in your room as if you were on the ceiling looking down.

The FOUR DIRECTIONS
The Way to Go!

Maps help us get where we want to go. They show us which **direction**, or which way, to take. Maps have four main directions. They are **north**, **south**, **east**, and **west**.

North and South

- **Find the arrows that show north and south on the map.**
- **Which one points up? Which one points down?**

East and West

- **Find the arrows that show east and west.**
- **Which one points to the right? Which one points to the left?**

Follow Directions

The key on a map tells the meaning of each symbol.

- **Use the key to find the playground and the flower garden.**
- **Trace the path from the playground to the garden. In what direction did you go?**

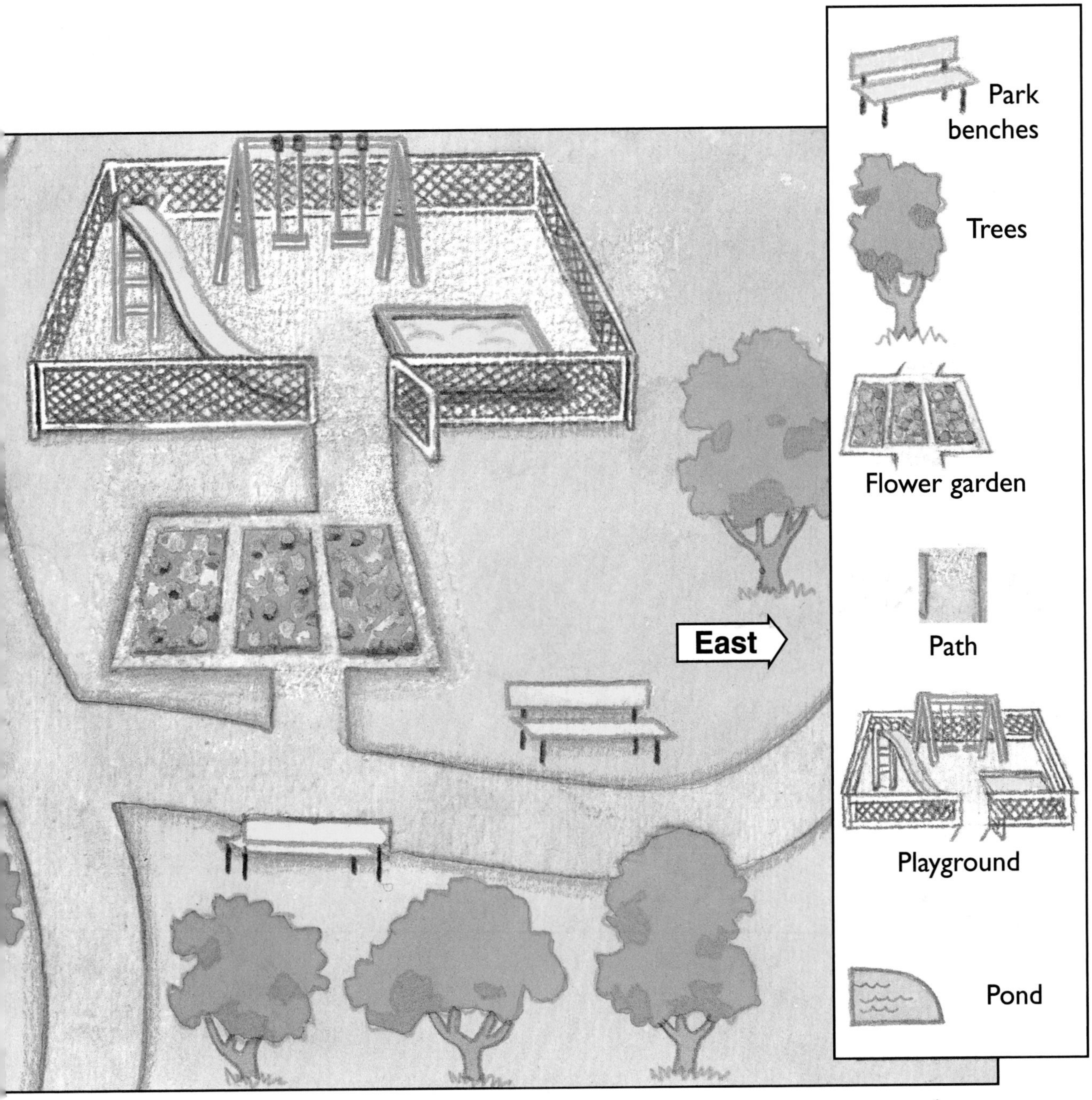

Park
benches

Trees

Flower garden

East

Path

Playground

Pond

Now Try This!

Draw a map of a desert island.
Use arrows to show the four
directions on your map.

Looking at FLOOR PLANS

A **floor plan** is a map of a room. It looks like a drawing that someone made looking down from the ceiling. It shows the shape of the room and where things are. The floor plan on these pages shows the children's room at a library.

How Things Shape Up

Floor plans show the shapes of things.

- **The map key tells the meaning of each symbol. Use the key to find the librarian's desk.**
- **What shape is it?**

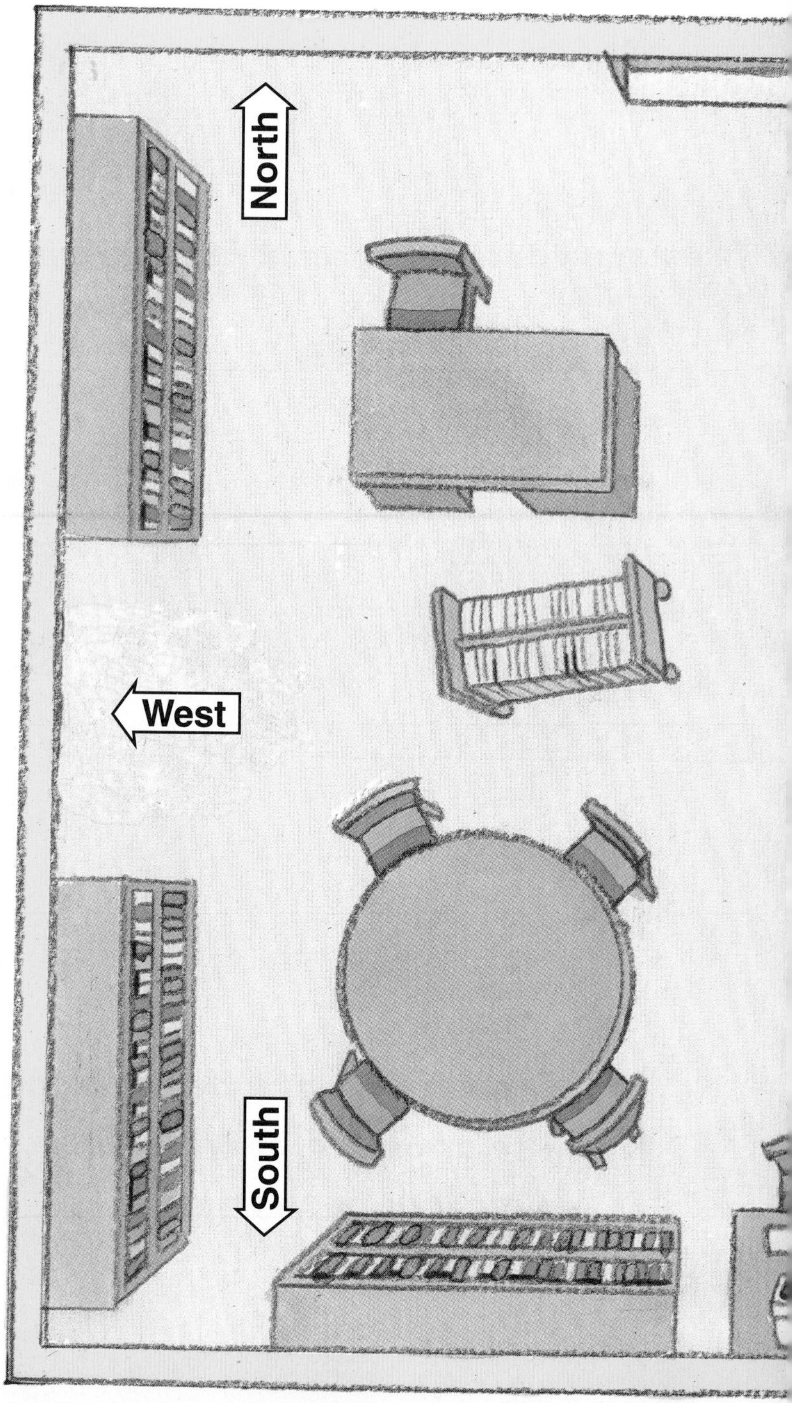

Finding What You Need

- **Find a place where you could pick out a book.**
- **You are doing a project with three classmates. Find a place where you can work together.**

North

West

South

Finding Your Way Around

- **Start at the book cart and walk east.**
- **Where did you go?**

 **Bookcase**

 **Computer**

 **Book cart**

 **Table**

 Librarian's desk

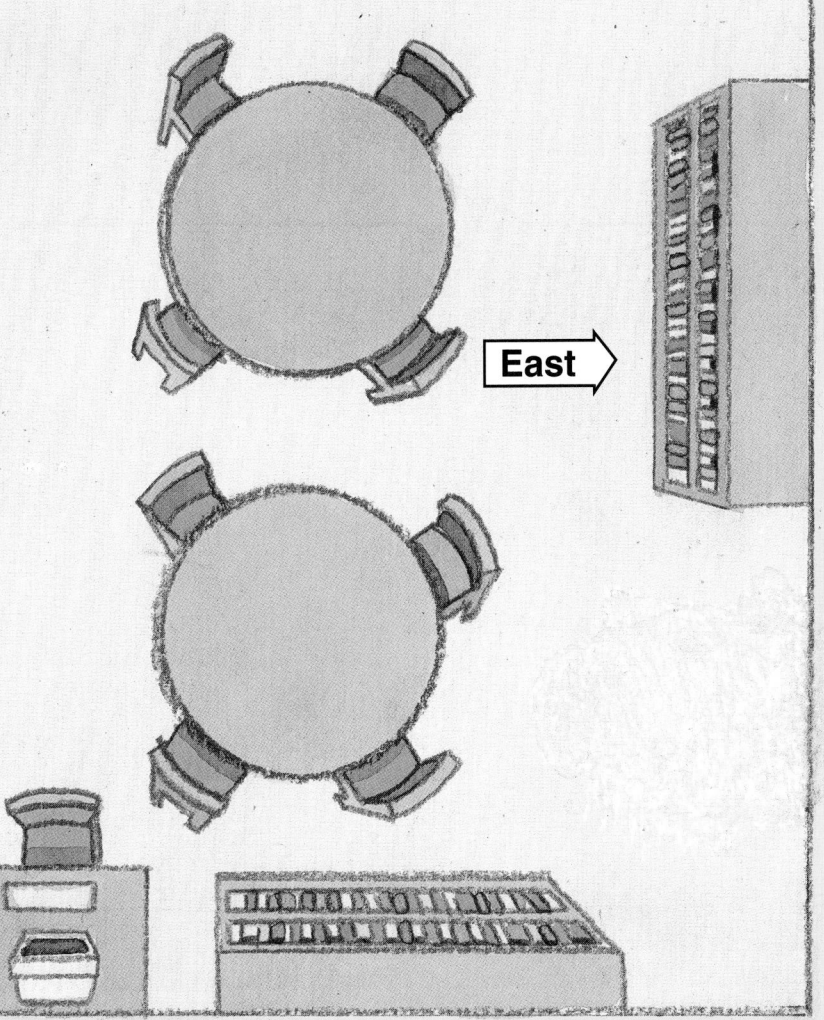

East

Now Try This!

Cut out pieces of paper in the shapes of the things in the floor plan. Put them on a piece of paper in the same way they're shown on the floor plan. Then put them down your own way. How is your floor plan different?

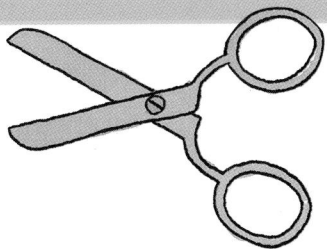

M9

How to READ a MAP

Maps tell us many things, such as where a place is and how to get there. Without maps, we'd really be lost! The map on these pages shows all 50 states of our country. Read the map to learn about the United States.

What is an **abbreviation**? It's a shortened form of a word. Mapmakers often use abbreviations for the names of the states.

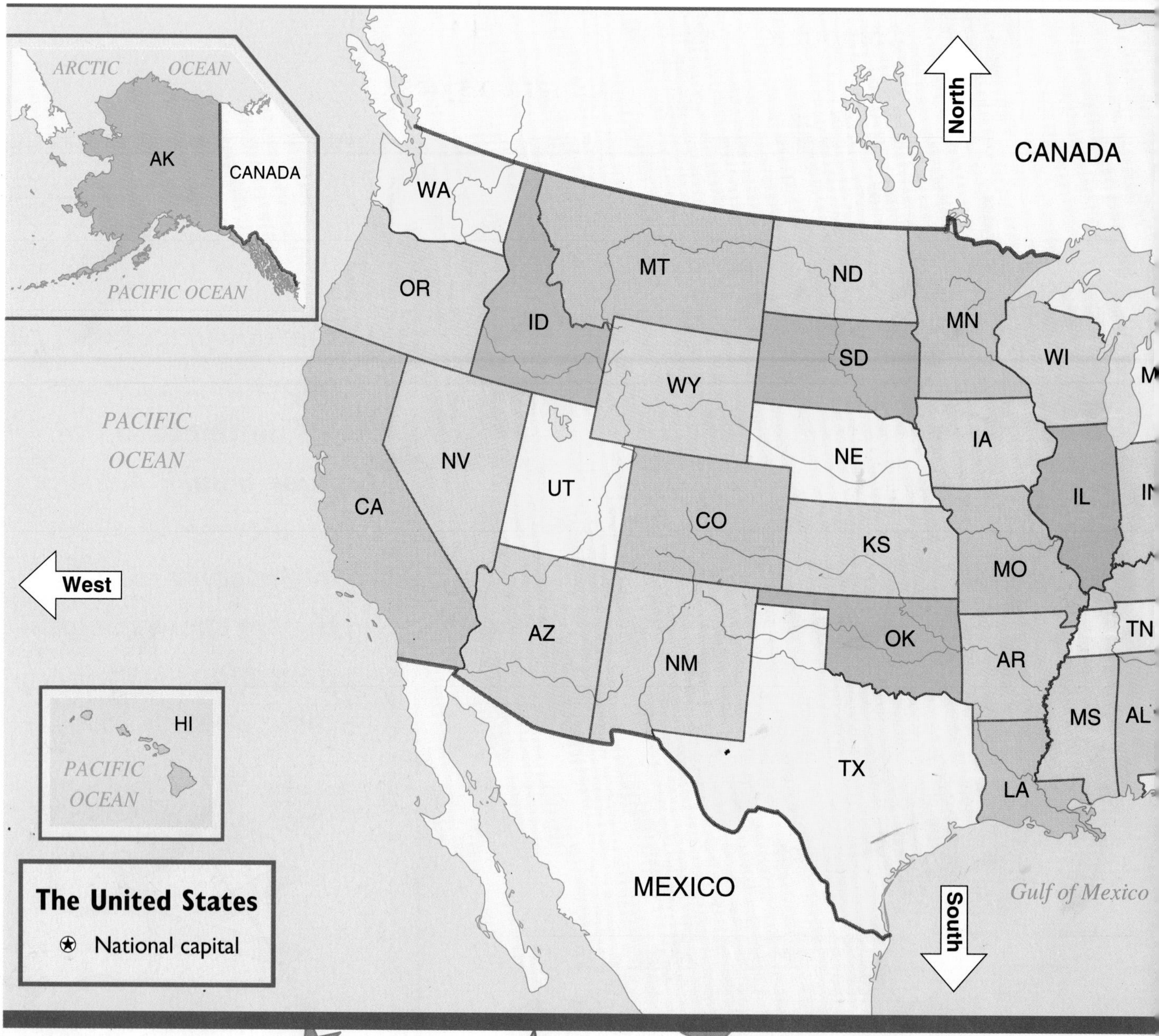

Map with the following labels:

ARCTIC OCEAN

AK

CANADA

PACIFIC OCEAN

North

CANADA

WA

OR

MT

ND

MN

WI

M

ID

SD

WY

IA

IL

IN

PACIFIC OCEAN

NV

UT

NE

CO

KS

MO

TN

CA

West

AZ

OK

AR

MS

AL

NM

HI

PACIFIC OCEAN

TX

LA

MEXICO

South

Gulf of Mexico

The United States

⊛ National capital

There's No Place Like Home!

- **Find the state where you live on the map.**

- **Do other states touch your state? What are their names?**

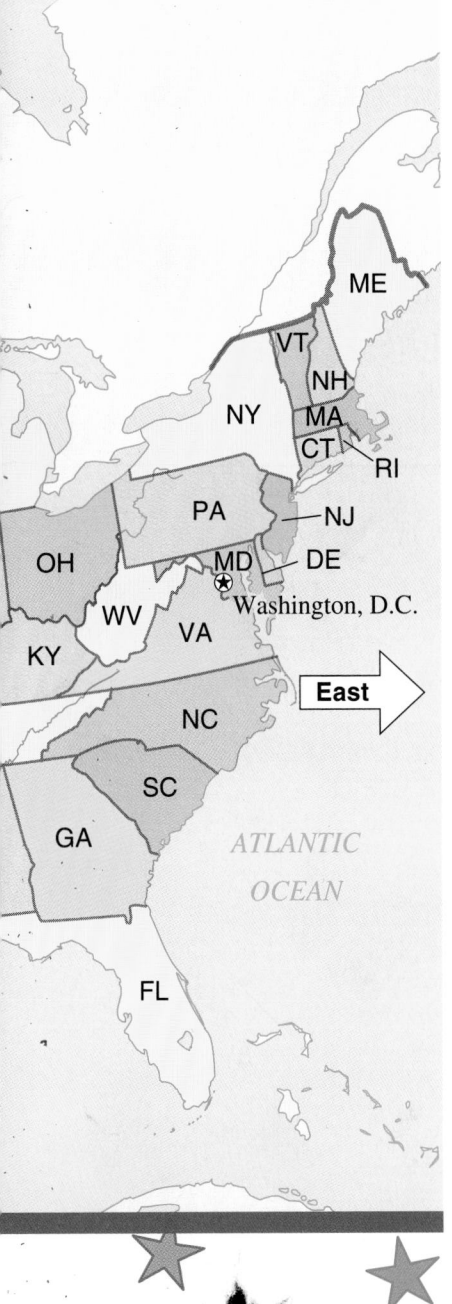

ME

VT

NH

NY   MA
      CT
           RI

PA   NJ

OH   MD   DE
             ✩
WV   Washington, D.C.

VA

KY

→ **East**

NC

SC

GA   ATLANTIC
      OCEAN

FL

Alabama	AL
Alaska	AK
Arizona	AZ
Arkansas	AR
California	CA
Colorado	CO
Connecticut	CT
Delaware	DE
Florida	FL
Georgia	GA
Hawaii	HI
Idaho	ID
Illinois	IL
Indiana	IN
Iowa	IA
Kansas	KS
Kentucky	KY
Louisiana	LA
Maine	ME
Maryland	MD
Massachusetts	MA
Michigan	MI
Minnesota	MN
Mississippi	MS
Missouri	MO
Montana	MT
Nebraska	NE
Nevada	NV
New Hampshire	NH
New Jersey	NJ
New Mexico	NM
New York	NY
North Carolina	NC
North Dakota	ND
Ohio	OH
Oklahoma	OK
Oregon	OR
Pennsylvania	PA
Rhode Island	RI
South Carolina	SC
South Dakota	SD
Tennessee	TN
Texas	TX
Utah	UT
Vermont	VT
Virginia	VA
Washington	WA
West Virginia	WV
Wisconsin	WI
Wyoming	WY

Two Letters, Please!

- **Look at the list. Find the name of your state.**

- **What letters are in its short form?**

Seacoast States

- **You want to find an ocean beach. Name six states where you could go.**

Now Try This!

Pick five states. Write their names on five slips of paper. Ask a classmate to do the same thing. Then take turns picking a slip. Ask your partner what the abbreviation is for that state.

M11

Learning About CONTINENTS and OCEANS

Earth is covered by large land areas and huge areas of salty water. We call the land areas **continents**. The areas of salty water are **oceans**. Look at the map on these pages to learn about the world's continents and oceans.

A different color is used to show each continent. The color blue is used to show oceans.

The World's Water

- **Read the names of the four oceans.**
- **Find the Indian Ocean. What land does it touch?**
- **Go from Africa to Australia. What ocean will you cross?**

The World's Land

- **How many continents are there?**
- **Name each continent as you point to it.**

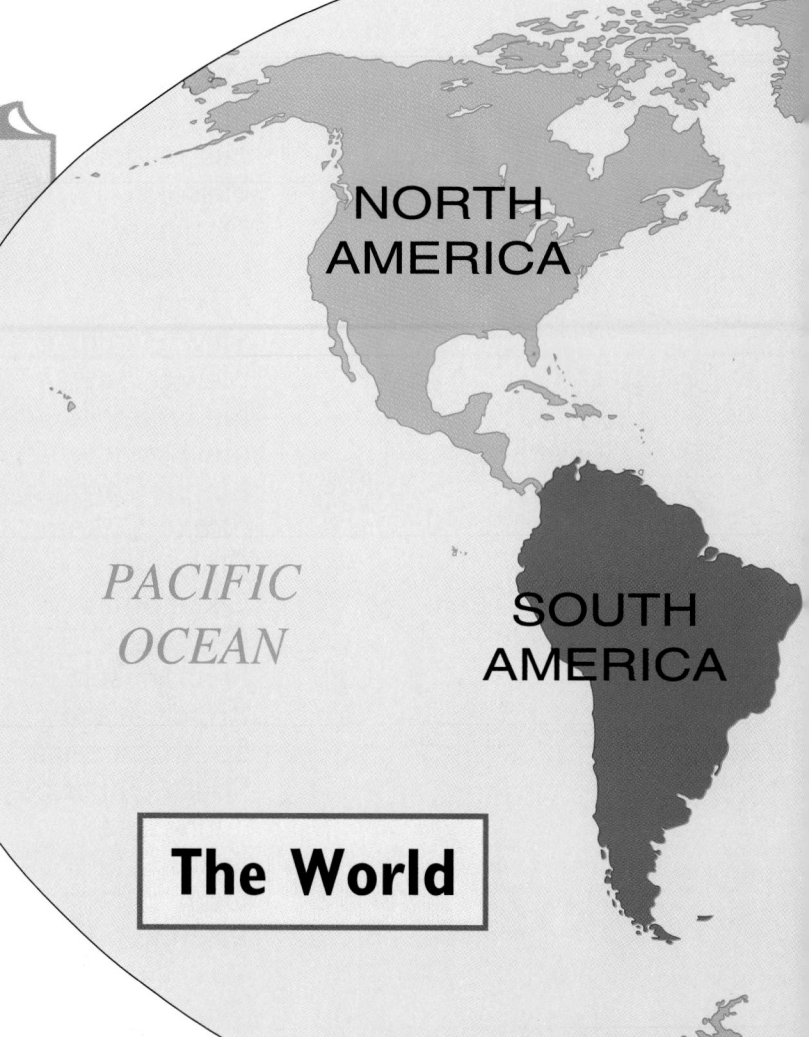

NORTH AMERICA

SOUTH AMERICA

PACIFIC OCEAN

The World

We Live Here!

Our country is on the continent of North America.

- Trace the outline of North America with your finger.
- What continent is below North America?
- What oceans touch South America?

Now Try This!

Plan a trip around the world. Go to every continent and cross every ocean. Start from North America. List each ocean and continent as you reach it.

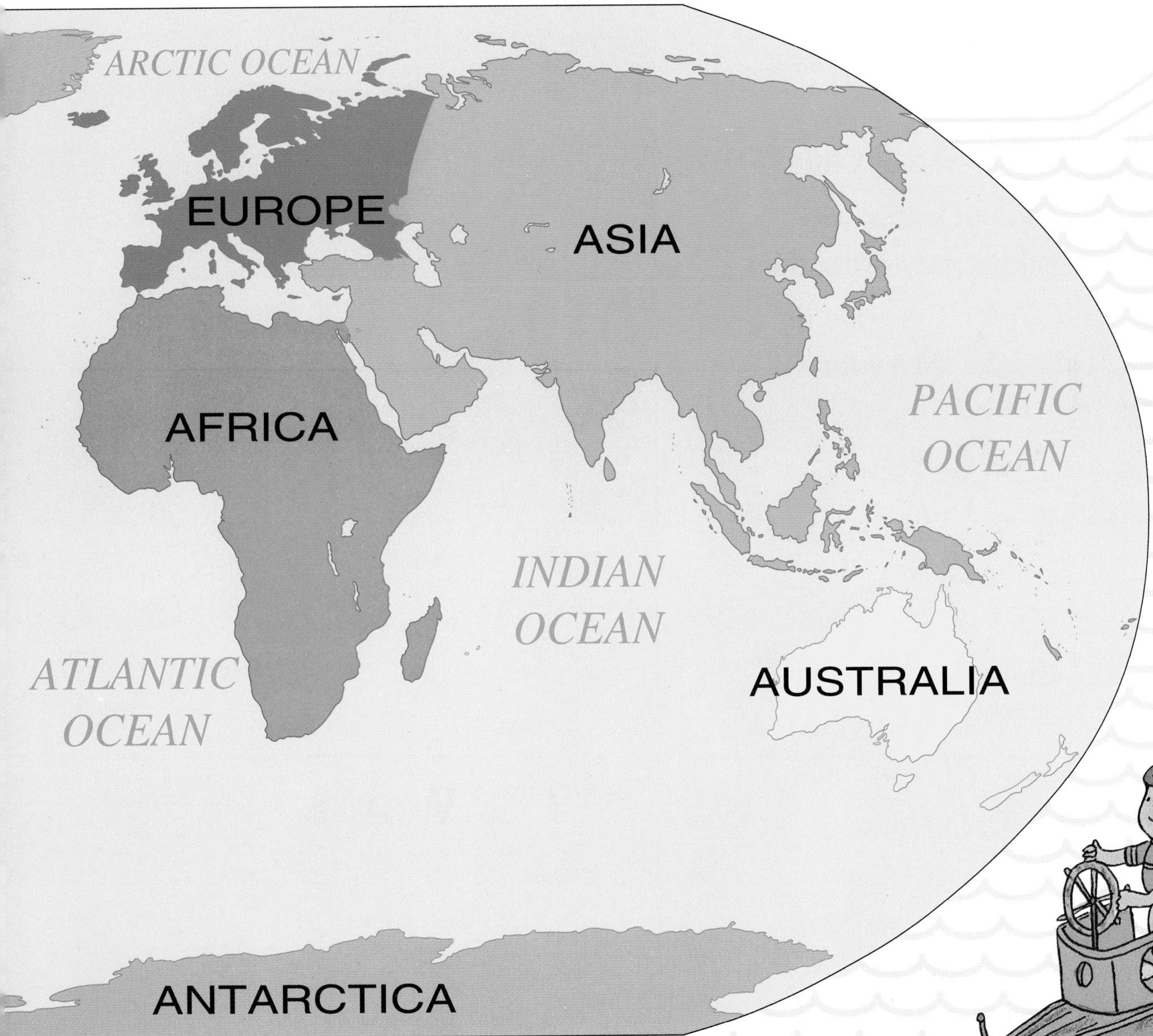

ARCTIC OCEAN

EUROPE

ASIA

AFRICA

PACIFIC OCEAN

INDIAN OCEAN

ATLANTIC OCEAN

AUSTRALIA

ANTARCTICA

Bodies of WATER, Kinds of LAND

Earth's surface is covered by land and water. There are many different bodies of water on Earth. There are many different kinds of land, too. The drawing on these pages shows a few of the bodies of water and kinds of land on Earth.

Big Differences

An **ocean** is a huge body of salt water.

- Find an ocean in the drawing.

A **lake** is a body of water with land almost all the way around it.

- Find a lake. Trace the edge or shore of the lake with your finger.

Moving Along

A **river** is a long body of running water. A river usually flows into a lake or an ocean.

- Find a river. Then trace its path.
- Does the river flow into another body of water?

Desert

No Umbrellas Needed!

A desert is a hot and dry area of land. It gets very little rain.

- Find a desert. How is it different from the land around the lake?

On Top of the World

A mountain is very high land. It rises much higher than the land around it.

- Point to a mountain in the picture.
- How many mountains are there? Count the peaks.

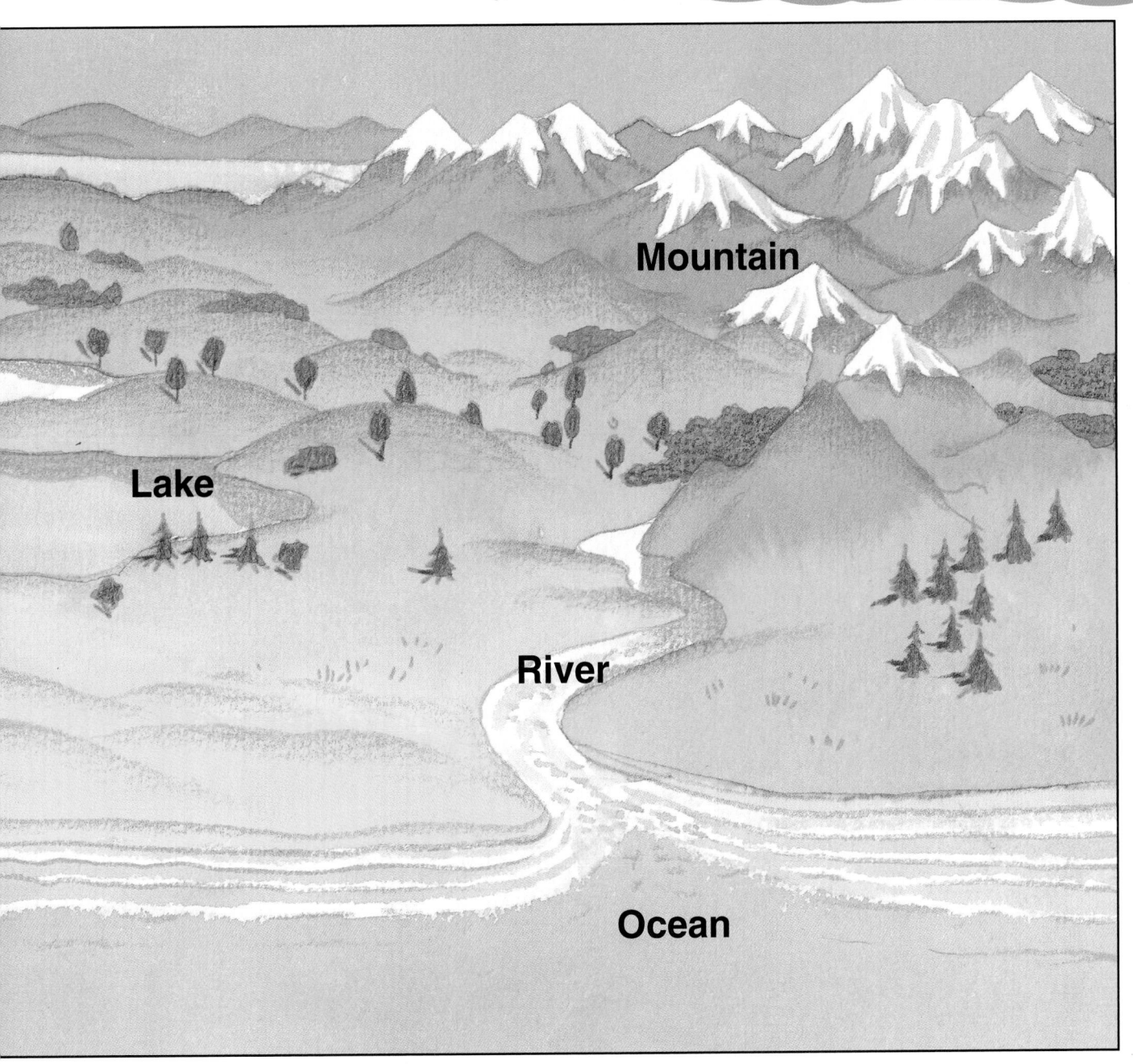

Mountain

Lake

River

Ocean

Rules and Laws

The Rules of the Road

The signs you see are telling you
Important rules you need to do.
"Please turn around. This street's one way!"
"Ride your bike here. It's okay."
"Walk/Don't Walk" and "No U-Turn"
Are other rules you need to learn.
Now think of other signs you see,
Because they're meant for your safety!

NO DOGS ALLOWED

Theme 1

Rules

▼ Why is this boy holding up his arm? Find out on page 13.

There are all kinds of rules to follow in school, at home, and in a community. When everyone follows the rules, we can get along, be safe, and have fun.

CONTENTS

and Laws

These books are about the importance of rules and laws. Read one that interests you and fill out a book-review form.

READ AND FIND OUT

Dinosaurs, Beware!: A Safety Guide
by Marc Brown and Stephen Krensky
(Little, Brown & Co., 1982)
The dinosaurs in this book have a lot to learn about safety. Find out what happens to them in the kitchen, on the playground, and during the night.

Manners **by Aliki** (William Morrow & Co., 1990)
Boys and girls with good manners are fun to be with. This book will help you think about your own manners and those of people you know.

Emergency! **by Gail Gibbons**
(Holiday House, 1994)
Some community helpers use special kinds of vehicles and equipment to help others when there is an emergency. You can even read about helpers of long ago.

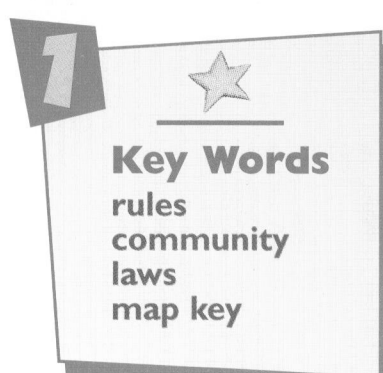

Let's Go by the Rules!

1

Key Words
rules
community
laws
map key

Rules to Follow

Hi! My name is Rachel Rule. Did you ever think about all the **rules** that you follow each day? Everyone has rules to follow, such as looking both ways before crossing a street. There are rules that help us at home, at school, and in the **community**. A community is a place where people live, work, and play. Come along with me to see some of the rules I follow in just one day.

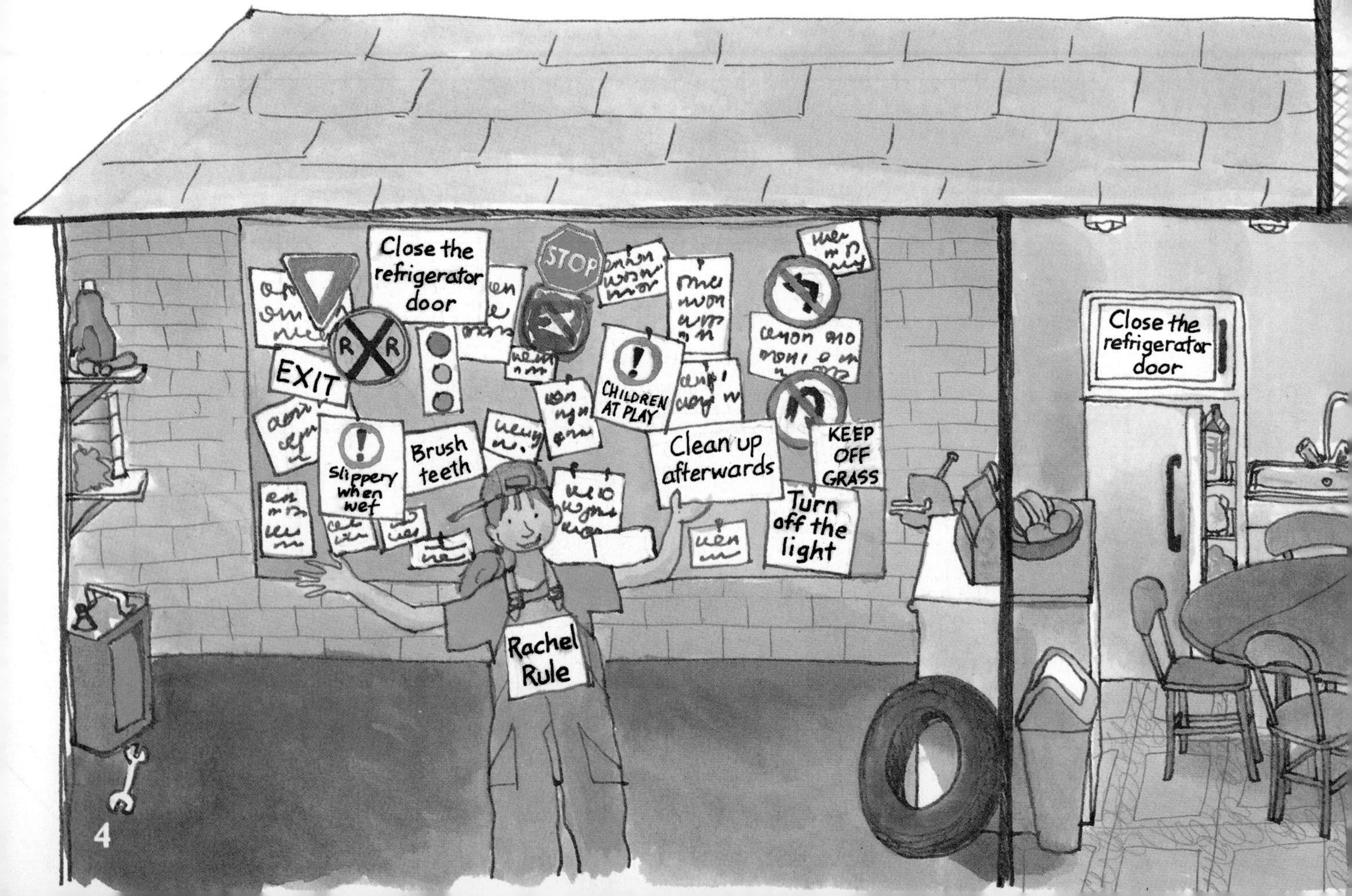

Close the refrigerator door
STOP
R R
EXIT
CHILDREN AT PLAY
Slippery when wet
Brush teeth
Clean up afterwards
KEEP OFF GRASS
Turn off the light
Rachel Rule
Close the refrigerator door

Rules at Home

My day starts off in the morning with my family—Mr. and Mrs. Rule (that's my mom and dad), Richie (that's my brother), and me. At home we have many rules that we should know. But Richie sometimes forgets, so I leave him reminder notes around the house. Can you spot all the rules we have at our house?

Rules in the Community

After I leave my house in the morning, I walk to my school. The rules I must follow in my community are called laws. One law is to stop at stop signs. Another law is to throw away trash in baskets. Laws help keep people safe. They also help keep our community clean and nice. What laws do you follow in your community?

6

Rules at School

In school we decided on some rules to make things better in our classroom. One of our rules is to keep our books nice so that next year's class can enjoy them, too. But sometimes we forget the rules. Do you see the rules that are being broken in this picture?

MAP ADVENTURE

Rachel Rule's Community

Rachel's Community

The map shows places where laws are not being followed. Rachel's community is missing some important signs that tell what the laws are.

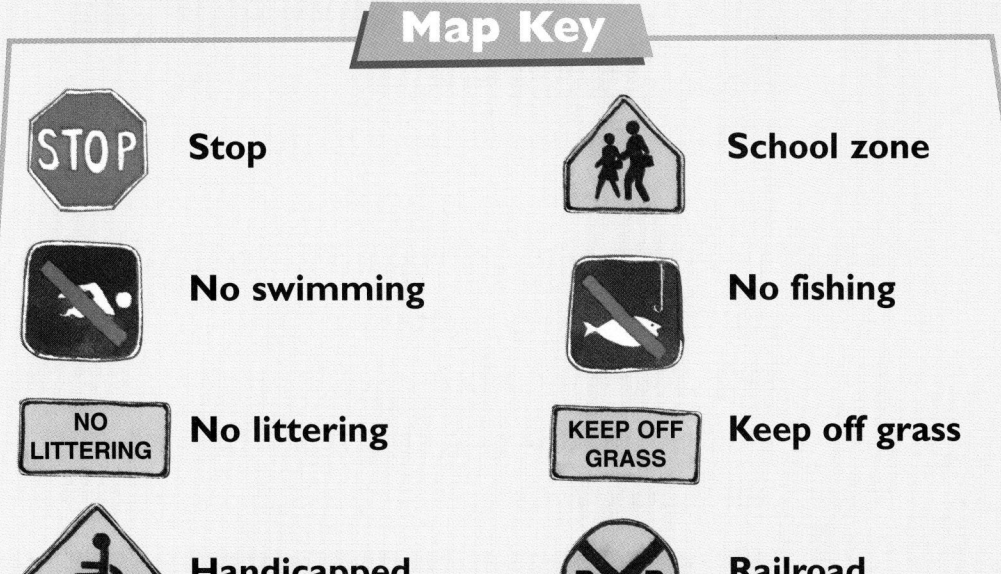

Map Key

Stop

School zone

No swimming

No fishing

No littering

Keep off grass

Handicapped crossing

Railroad crossing

SHOW WHAT YOU KNOW!

MAP IT

You can help the people in Rachel's community. First, look at the **map key**. A map key helps you understand a map. Then, find the places on this map where signs are missing. Finally, match the signs to the places where they are needed.

EXPLORE IT

Fold a piece of paper in half. On one half, draw one of the places from the map. On the other half, draw the sign that is needed and show the law being followed.

2

Key Word
protect

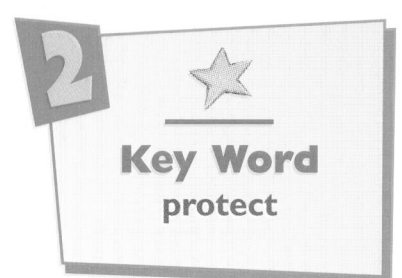

SAFETY FIRST

Police Officers Keep Us Safe

Meet Sharon Wilson and Jack Díaz. They are police officers who work together. Officers Wilson and Díaz drive through their community in a patrol car. They remind people to obey laws. Laws help make a community a safe place in which to live. Come along with the officers as they help keep people safe.

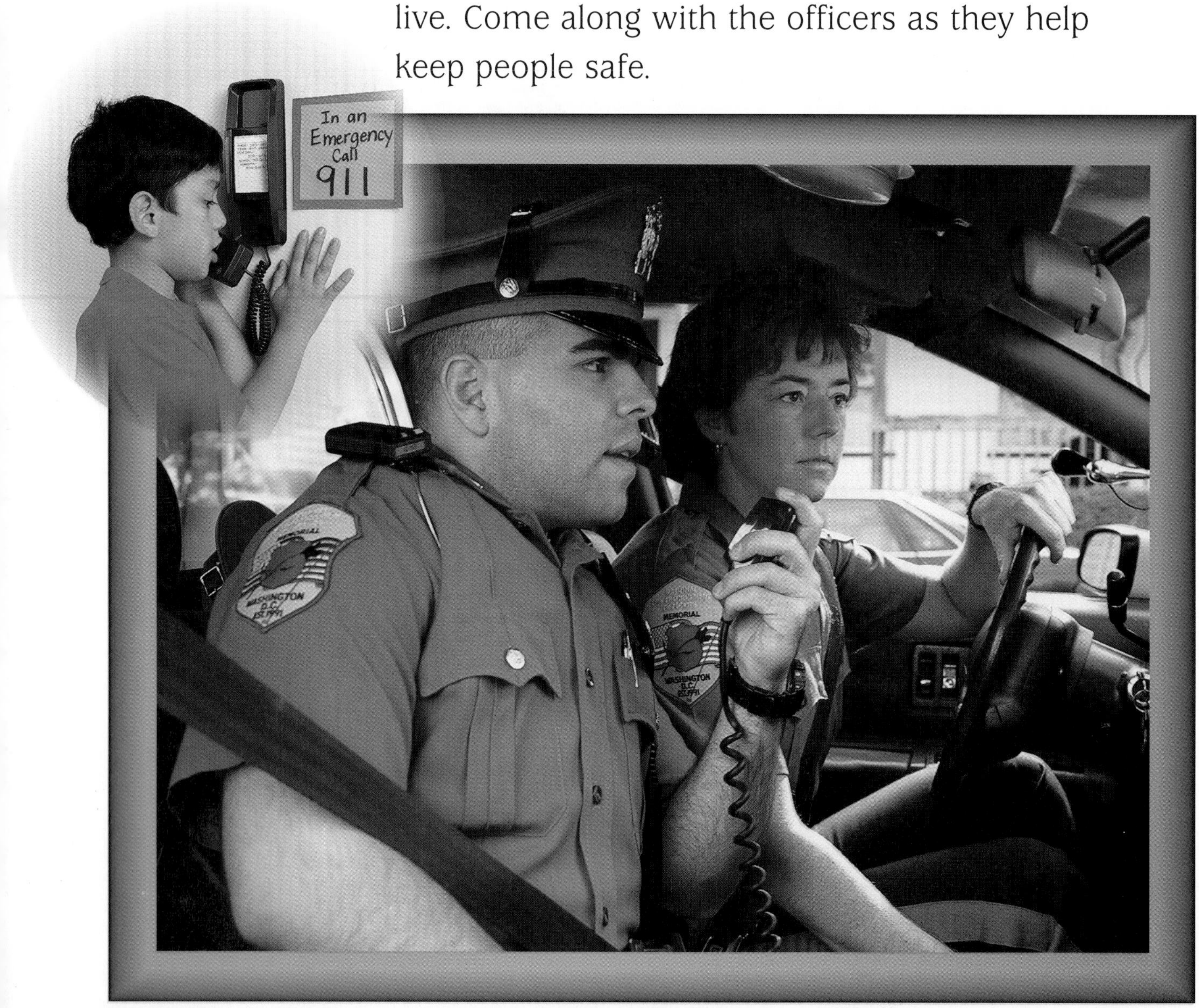
In an Emergency Call 911

Safety at Home

Officers Wilson and Díaz begin the day by answering a child's 911 call for help. The child's mother tripped on a toy left on the stairs. The officers and an emergency medical services worker take care of the mother. To prevent other accidents, the officers remind the child to keep toys off the stairs.

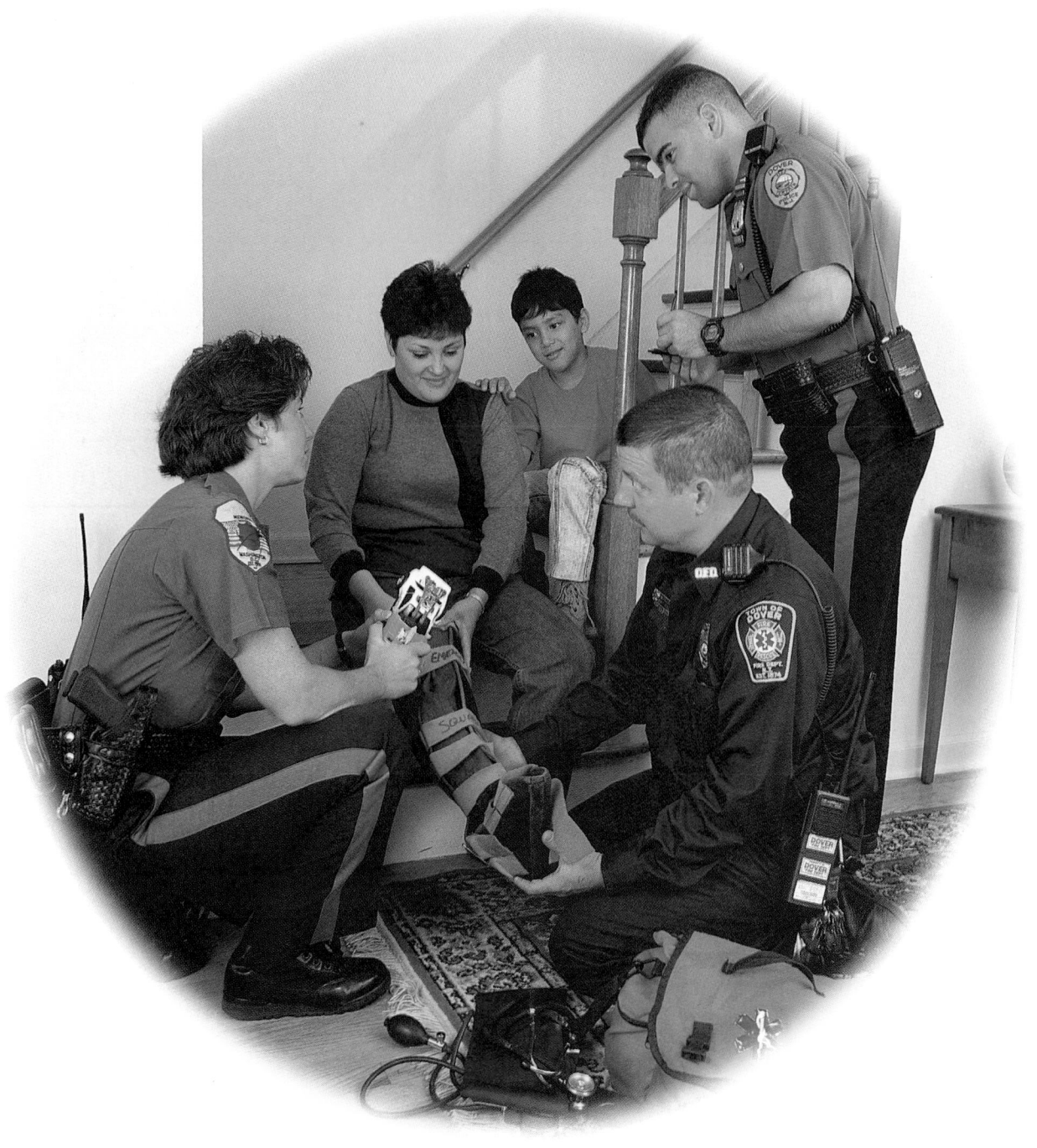

Safety in the Community

Later the officers help people who were in a car accident. Luckily no one was hurt. Everyone had been wearing seat belts. This is an important safety law. Officers Wilson and Díaz talk to each driver. In this way they gather information for an accident report.

◄ Officer Díaz shows the children the hand signal for a right-hand turn.

Bicycle Safety

In the afternoon the officers talk about bicycle safety to second graders. They share several safety tips, such as keeping bikes in good condition and using hand signals. They also talk about why people should wear bike helmets. Officer Díaz's safety message is "Please wear bike helmets. They will **protect** you from getting hurt."

SHOW WHAT YOU KNOW!

THINK AND WRITE ABOUT IT

Think of three safety rules—one for home, one for school, and one for your community. Write each rule on a bumper sticker.

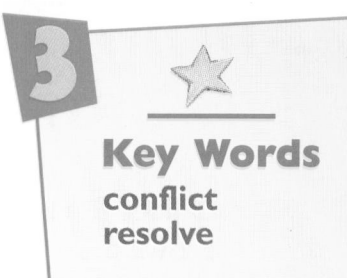
What Would You Do?

What Is a Conflict?

What would you do if a classmate pushed you off the swings? How would you feel if a friend tried to force you to do things his or her way? Each of these situations is called a **conflict**. Conflicts can cause you to feel uncomfortable. What can you do when a conflict happens?

A Playground Conflict

You and Betsy are friends. But at recess, Betsy pushed you because she wanted to be first on the swings. Her push made you fall down and hit your knee. Betsy knows that pushing is against school rules, but she hasn't said that she's sorry. What would you do?

Using Your Words

Before you ask for your teacher's help, try to **resolve**, or find an answer to, the conflict yourself. You may feel like pushing Betsy back, but that won't resolve the conflict. It may even make matters worse!

Try using your words to tell Betsy how you feel. You might say, "I don't like being pushed. Please don't do that again." Try to work out a resolution, or an answer. One resolution could be to take turns on the swings. Can you think of another?

Friends Have Conflicts

Kareem just told you that he won't be your best friend any longer unless you let him pitch. Kareem isn't being fair. He always pitches. You don't want to lose him as a friend. But giving in to Kareem doesn't feel like the right thing to do. What else can you do?

Resolve Your Conflicts

A good friend shouldn't try to force you to do things his or her way. You might explain to Kareem that friends share and take turns. Let him know how you feel. You might say, "I feel hurt when you tell me that you don't want to be my friend anymore." Then you might take turns pitching or flip a coin to see who pitches first. Can you think of another way to resolve this conflict?

Learn From Conflicts

Remember, you can learn from your conflicts. If you think you could have resolved a conflict in a better way, try it out the next time.

SHOW WHAT YOU KNOW!

THINK AND TALK ABOUT IT

A friend wants to play with your sister's computer. But she isn't home. You explain the rule that your sister must be with you when you use her computer. Your friend says, "Don't worry, she won't know." What should you do now?

Key Word
custom

A World of Customs

The Custom of Saying Hello

Greetings! Did you know that there are many ways to greet people you meet? A handshake, a hug, and a smile are ways to say hello. The way that people say hello is an important **custom**. A custom is a group's special way of doing something.

In the state of Hawaii, it is a custom to say "Aloha," which means "hello." In Japan, people bow when they meet. And many people who cannot hear use their hands to sign, or say, hello.

Look at the flags on the map. They will help you find the places that you will read about in this lesson.

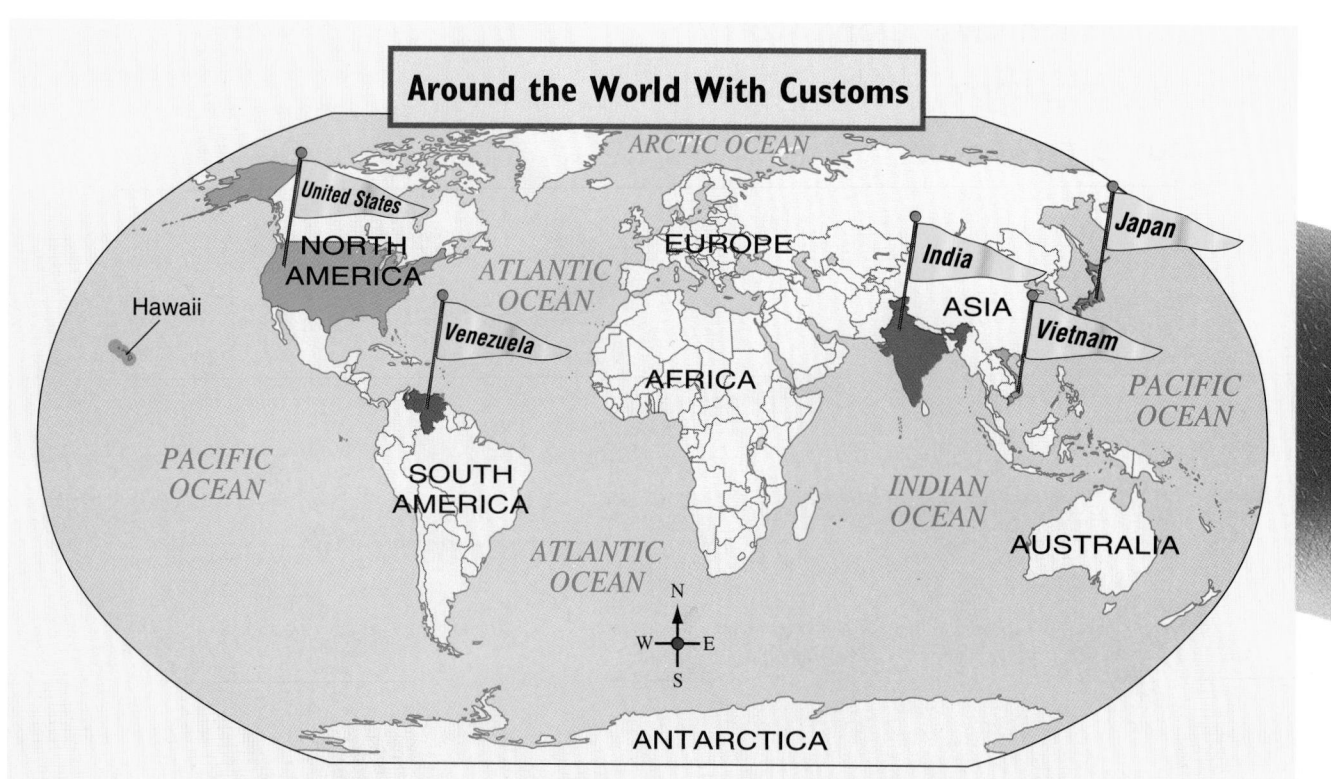

Around the World With Customs

ARCTIC OCEAN

United States

NORTH AMERICA

Hawaii

ATLANTIC OCEAN

EUROPE

India

ASIA

Japan

Vietnam

Venezuela

AFRICA

PACIFIC OCEAN

PACIFIC OCEAN

SOUTH AMERICA

INDIAN OCEAN

AUSTRALIA

ATLANTIC OCEAN

N
W E
S

ANTARCTICA

The Custom of Being Polite

Being polite is also an important custom. In the United States, people usually stand at least two feet apart when talking. In Venezuela, people often stand closer together.

In Vietnam it is the custom to use only the right hand or both hands to pass an object. In India it is not polite to use the left hand to eat. What are some customs for politeness in the United States?

▼ This boy is using his hand to sign, or say, hello.

Customs at Home

Families share many kinds of customs at home. Some families enjoy eating pizza together on Friday nights. Other families enjoy reading books or playing games on weekends. What are some customs that you enjoy at home?

Meal Customs

Can you think of different ways that people eat their food? Sometimes we use knives, forks, and spoons. Or we might use chopsticks to eat. At other times we use our hands to pick up food, such as a hot dog or a taco. What are some meal customs that you share with your family?

Customs We Share

People share many kinds of customs. What are customs you share with your classmates at school? Can you think of customs that many Americans share? We share customs at home, in our communities, in our country, and around the world. No matter where we live, our customs are special to us.

SHOW WHAT YOU KNOW!

THINK ABOUT IT AND DRAW IT

Fold a piece of paper in half. Then draw a family custom on one half and a meal custom on the other.

The News

A Citizen in Action!

Make A Difference Day

Did you ever think that one person could make a difference? Making a difference means doing a good deed for your community. Do you think that you can make a difference, too? Many people across the United States have answered yes by celebrating Make A Difference Day. Each October, people are invited to spend a day helping others. The map on this page shows some of the places where people helped and the ways they made a difference.

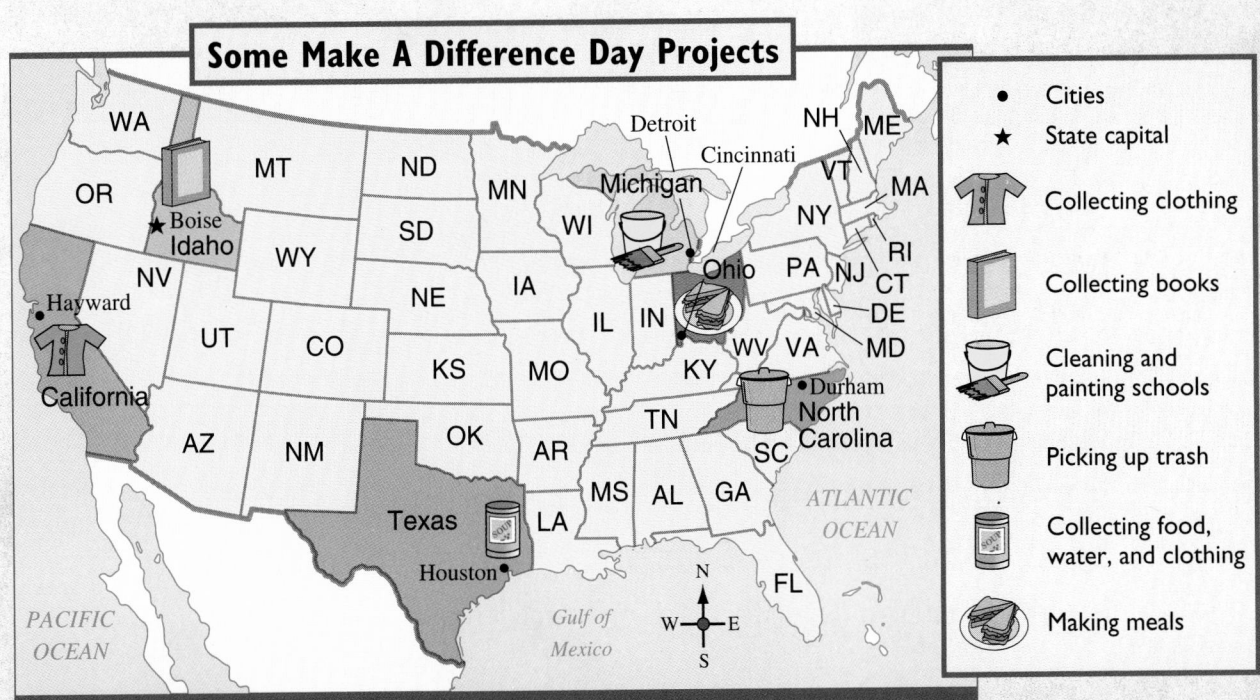

Some Make A Difference Day Projects

- Cities
- ★ State capital
- Collecting clothing
- Collecting books
- Cleaning and painting schools
- Picking up trash
- Collecting food, water, and clothing
- Making meals

Someone Who Made a Difference

Michael John Kelly from Hayward, California, is one person who made a difference. When Michael was eight years old, he collected two truckloads of clothing and other items from people in his community. He gave everything to homeless people. This was important to Michael because he and his mother had been homeless at one time. He wanted to help others because other people had helped him.

How a Good Deed Was Done

First, Michael began his good deed by writing a letter. In it he asked for clothing, toys, and other items. Next, he copied the letter and delivered it to many people. Then his mother helped by asking people to give things they didn't need. Last, Michael collected more than 50 bags of clothing and a truckload of furniture, dishes, and toys.

Being a Good Citizen

Today, Michael is older, but he is still helping others. On Saturdays he works in a food pantry. A food pantry is a place where food is collected and given to those who need it. Michael has found out that helping people has made a difference in his life, too. It makes him feel good about himself. Taking responsibility is one way to be a good **citizen**, or member of a country.

SHOW WHAT YOU KNOW!

THINK ABOUT IT AND MAKE A DIFFERENCE

Be a citizen in action! You can make a get-well card or help someone. Think of one thing you'd like to do for someone else today. Then do it!

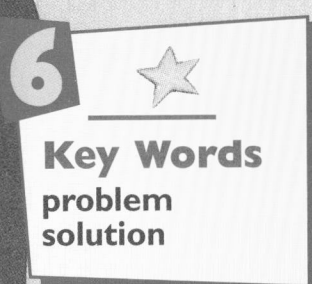

Let's Make a Difference

Working Together to Solve Problems

A few years ago, students in Glenwood, Maryland, were concerned about bicycle accidents in their community. They wanted to make bike riding safer. They began working together to solve this **problem**. Because of their hard work, they helped pass the first United States law requiring bike helmets.

Suppose that you and your classmates were concerned about safety when using in-line skates. Here are some steps that you and your classmates could follow to help solve the problem.

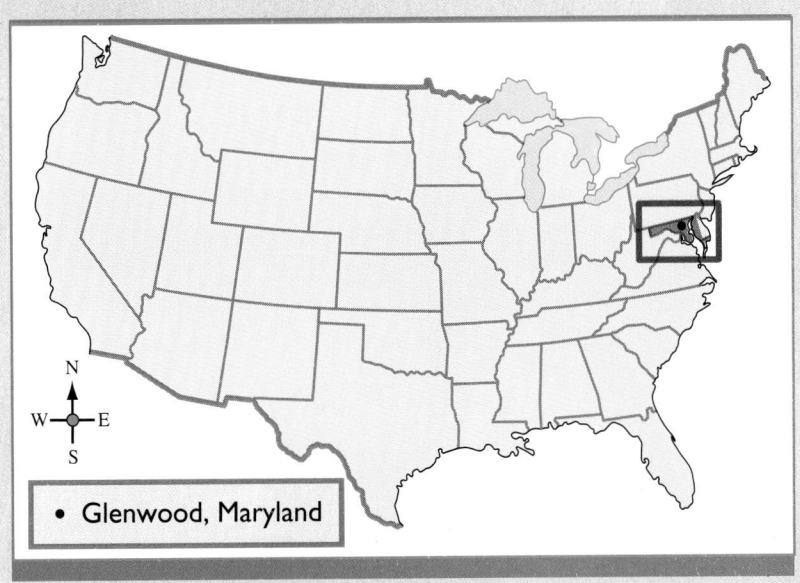

• Glenwood, Maryland

Step 1

Thinking About It

You and your classmates could meet with your teacher to discuss the problem. Then you could find information about skating accidents. For example, how many people in the United States have had this type of accident? In what ways did they get hurt? You could find the answers in your school or public library. Then you would have the information you need to plan a solution, or answer, to the problem.

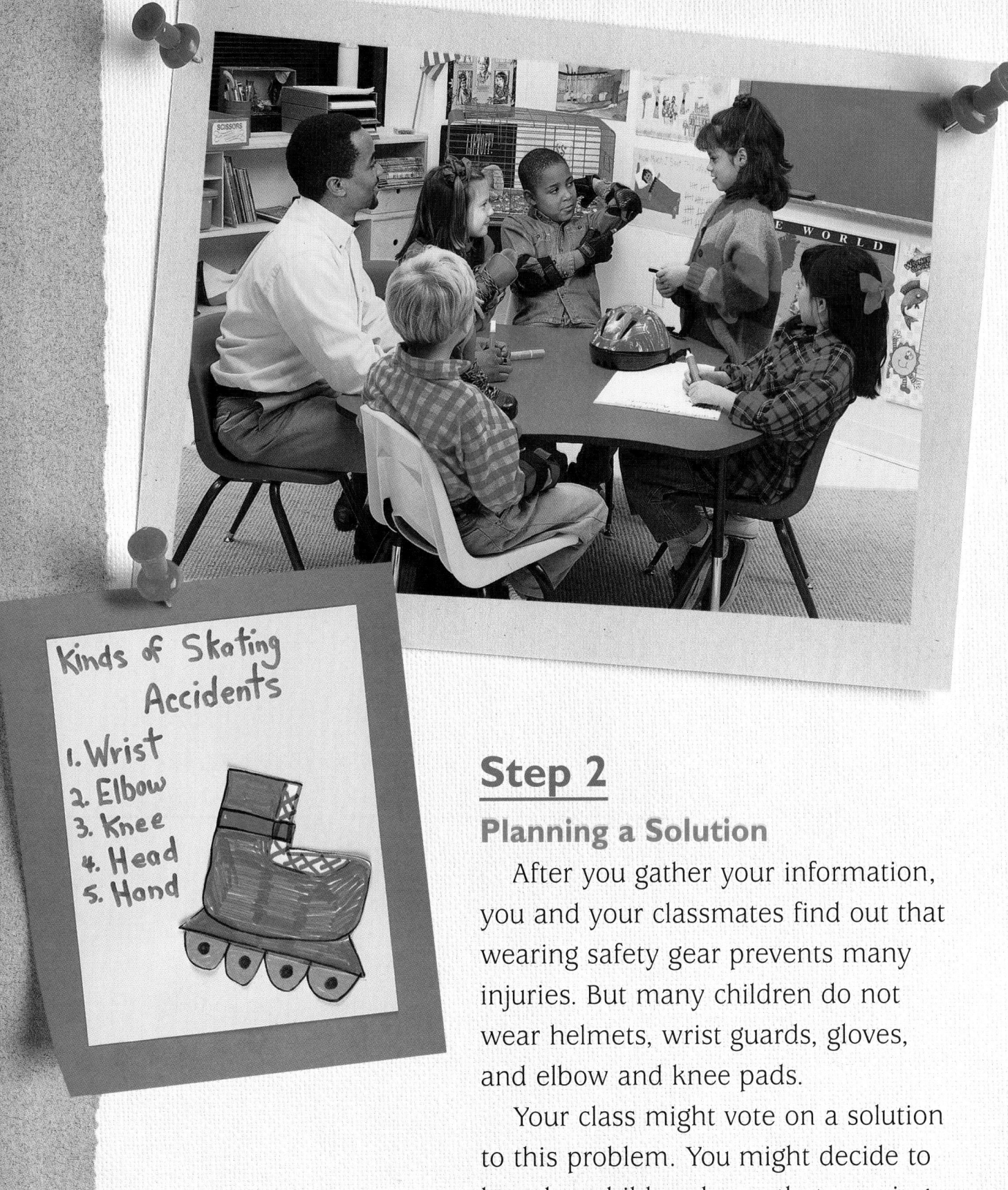

Kinds of Skating
Accidents

1. Wrist
2. Elbow
3. Knee
4. Head
5. Hand

Step 2

Planning a Solution

After you gather your information, you and your classmates find out that wearing safety gear prevents many injuries. But many children do not wear helmets, wrist guards, gloves, and elbow and knee pads.

Your class might vote on a solution to this problem. You might decide to let other children know that wearing safety gear is important.

31

The problem is solved. ▶

Because You
Are Dear,
Wear
Safety
Gear

Step 3

Solving the Problem

Your class could make posters and hang them up in school. These posters would remind everyone to wear safety gear when skating. Your class could also write letters to hand out to the people in your community.

Step 4

Sharing Your Ideas

Your class might meet with a lawmaker in your community. You can share your ideas about wearing safety gear. The lawmaker might agree to study the problem. You hope that this person will try to pass a new safety law. By working together, you can help solve a serious problem.

SHOW WHAT YOU KNOW!

THINK AND TALK ABOUT IT

Think of a classroom problem that needs to be solved. Plan a solution. Then share the problem and its solution with your classmates.

1 DO YOU REMEMBER . . .

1. Name two community laws that you read about.

2. What would you say to a first grader about bicycle safety?

3. Describe one way that you could resolve a conflict with a friend.

4. Name three different ways that people greet each other.

5. How did Michael help homeless people in his community?

6. What person in your community might you go to if you wanted to help solve a problem?

3 WHAT DO YOU THINK?

1. If you had a five-year-old brother, what four home rules would you want to help him remember?

2. Why do you think our country needs safety laws?

3. What would you do if you and a classmate both wanted the last piece of blue construction paper to finish making an American flag?

4. Describe a good deed you have done. How did it make you feel?

2 USING YOUR SKILLS

Describe the steps you would take to solve a problem. Look at the following steps to help you.

Problem-Solving Steps
1. Think about it
2. Plan a solution
3. Solve the problem
4. Share ideas

4 USING YOUR WORDS

Here is a story starter for you! Use at least five words from this list in your story.

Once upon a time, there were two friends named Julie and Kevin. They lived in a community where _____.

citizen	laws	resolve
conflict	problem	rules
custom	protect	solution

5 YOU CAN READ MAPS

Look at the map key and map. There are four signs that picture laws that are needed in this community. Where would you put each sign?

STOP **Stop**	NO LITTERING **No littering**
DO NOT ENTER **Do not enter**	KEEP OFF GRASS **Keep off grass**

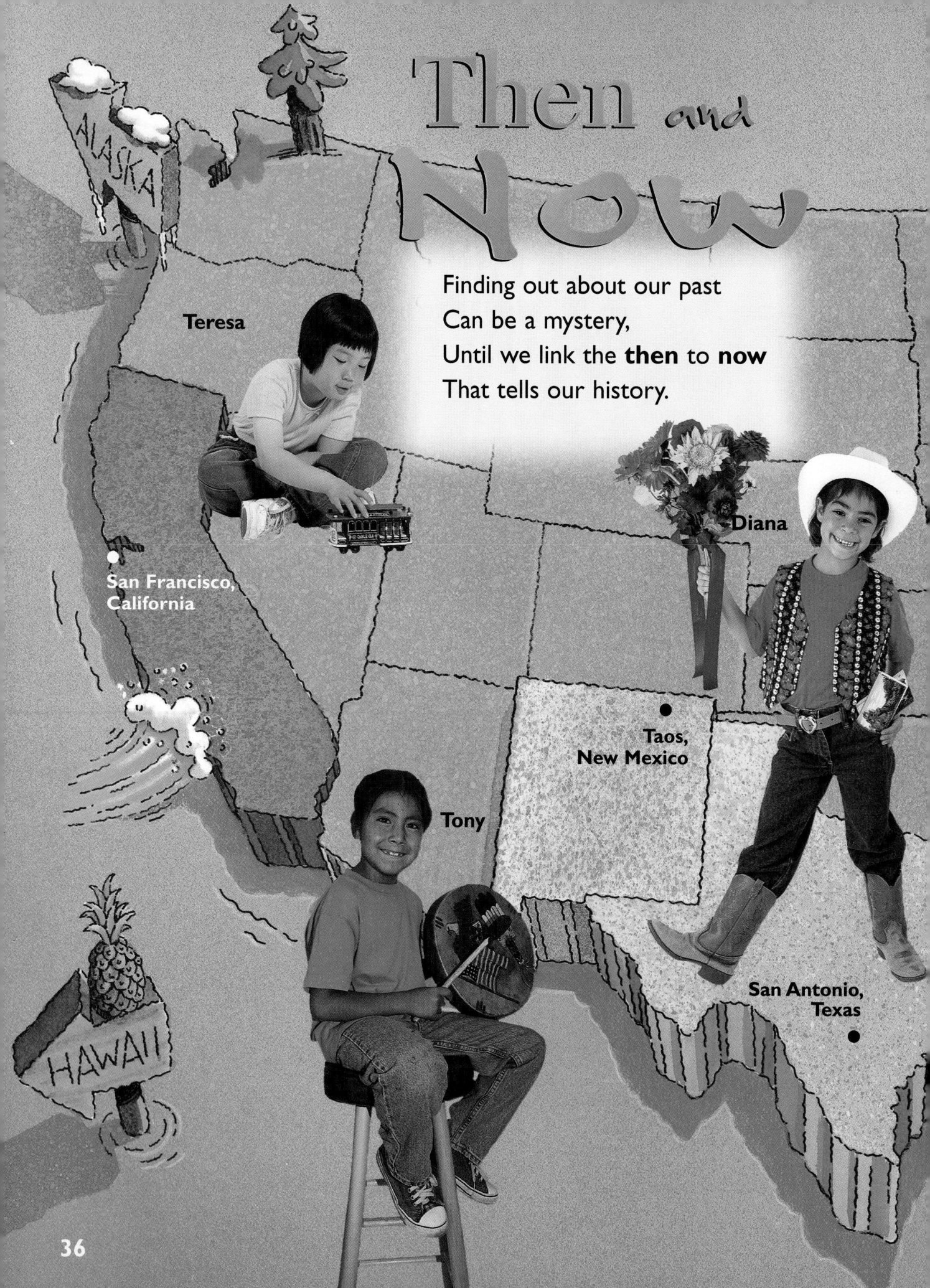

Then and Now

Finding out about our past
Can be a mystery,
Until we link the **then** to **now**
That tells our history.

ALASKA

Teresa

San Francisco,
California

Diana

Taos,
New Mexico

Tony

San Antonio,
Texas

HAWAII

36

Kim

Indianapolis,
Indiana

Williamsburg,
Virginia

Jack

Theme 2

Then *and*

▼ What do you think this boy is holding? Find out on page 48.

Did you know that you have your own history? Everyone does! There is also a history that our whole country shares. Learning about the past helps us understand who we are.

CONTENTS

Now

These books are about both the past and the present. Read one that interests you and fill out a book-review form.

READ AND FIND OUT

Who Came Down That Road? by George Ella Lyon, paintings by Peter Catalanotto
(Orchard Books, 1992)
When you walk on a path, do you ever wonder who has walked there before you? How would you like to follow a road that goes back to days of long ago?

Homeplace by Anne Shelby, illustrations by Wendy Anderson Halperin (Orchard Books, 1995)
Grandma tells her grandchild the story of their farmhouse and the relatives who lived in it through the years. The pictures will help you to see all the changes that took place.

Aunt Flossie's Hats (and Crab Cakes Later) by Elizabeth Fitzgerald Howard, paintings by James Ransome (Clarion Books, 1991)
Do you have a favorite relative who tells you stories? Sarah and Susan do. Their great-great-aunt Flossie has a story for each one of her hats.

My Family Album

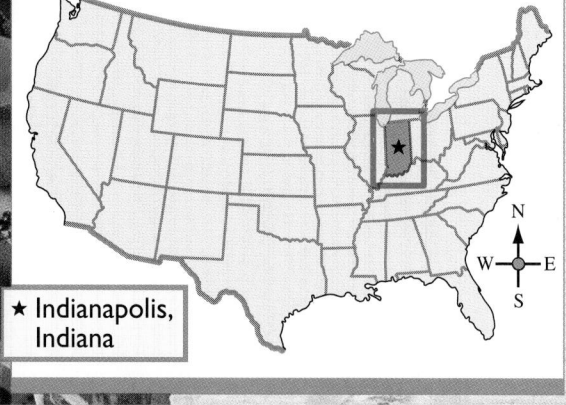

★ Indianapolis,
Indiana

Meet Kim

Hi! My name is Kim. I live with my family in the **city** of Indianapolis, Indiana. Many people live in this large community. My mother, father, sister, brother, and I live together in our house in Indianapolis.

When you look at the pictures in my family album, you will see how I've changed. One **change** you will see is how much bigger I am now than when I was younger. Now let's start at the beginning, when I was just a baby.

This is me today!

Kim in the Past

Everybody has a past. Here I am when I was little. I liked playing dress up. When I look at pictures from my past, they remind me of the ways I've changed. What changes do you see?

OPEN CHAMPIONSHIPS

THIRD PLACE

Kim in the Present

Here I am today. You can see that I am bigger now than I was in the past. I learned to ride a two-wheeler when I was six years old. Now my mom and I ride our bikes together. I also love to play soccer. My brother helped teach me to play. What are some ways you have changed?

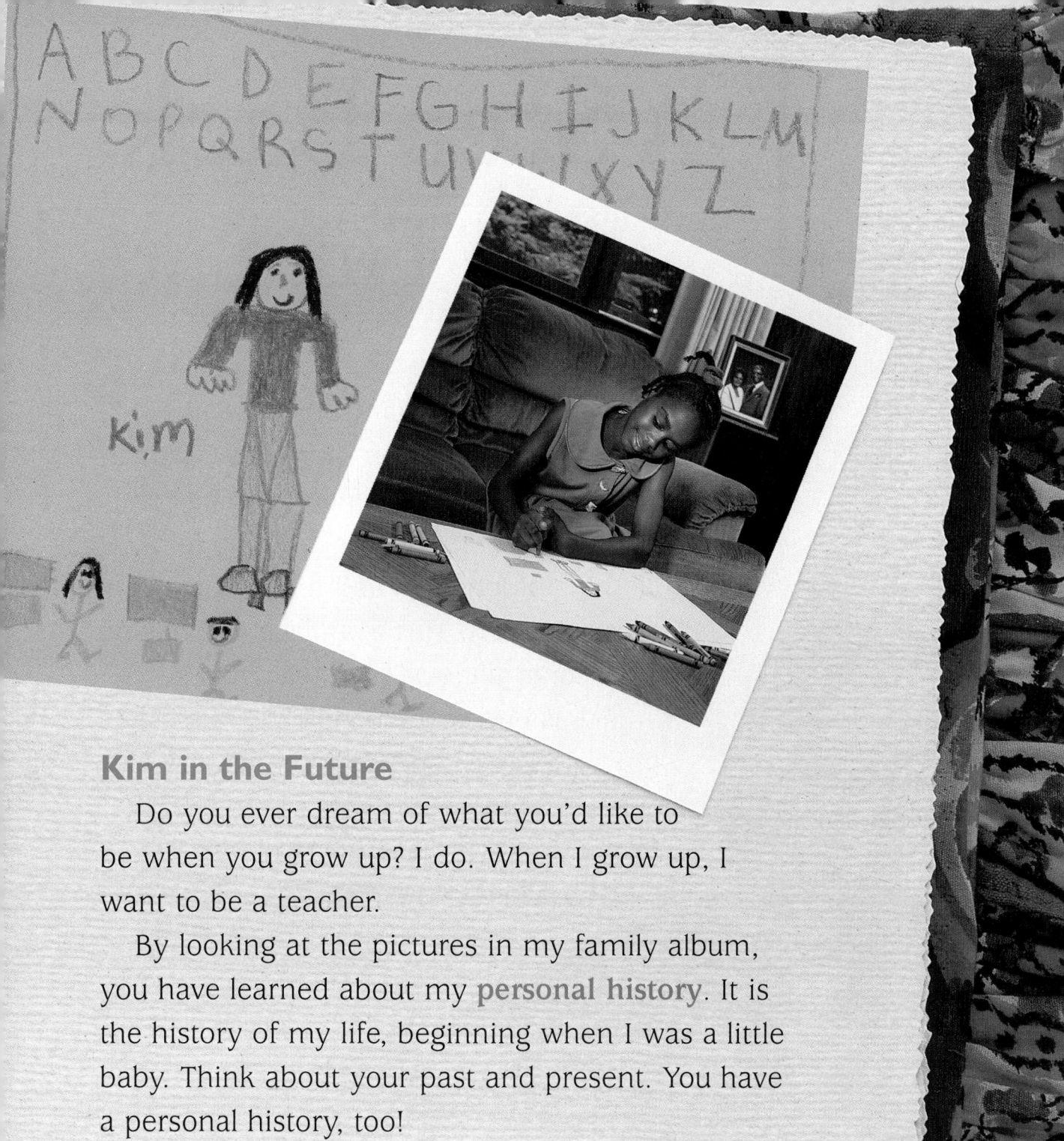

Kim in the Future

Do you ever dream of what you'd like to be when you grow up? I do. When I grow up, I want to be a teacher.

By looking at the pictures in my family album, you have learned about my **personal history**. It is the history of my life, beginning when I was a little baby. Think about your past and present. You have a personal history, too!

SHOW WHAT YOU KNOW!

DRAW IT AND WRITE ABOUT IT

Draw your own personal history—the story of your life. Fold a large piece of paper into three parts. Label the parts <u>past</u>, <u>present</u>, and <u>future</u>. Write a sentence and draw a picture for each part.

2

Key Words
history
apprentice

• Williamsburg,
Virginia

A Step Back in Time

Meet Jack Today

Jack lives in Williamsburg, Virginia. A special part of his community is Colonial Williamsburg. In this outdoor living-history museum, people dress up in clothing of long ago and tell visitors about the past. This is a place that has no cars, computers, or even telephones!

Jack is one of the people who dresses up. He tells visitors about the **history** of Williamsburg—how people lived in the past. Come with Jack to learn what life was like in the past.

Williamsburg

Map Key

Courthouse   Printer's Shop

Shoemaker's Shop

House

Market Square   Store

To Pond

Palace Street

Queen Street

Colonial Street

Duke of Gloucester Street

Waking Up in Williamsburg

Every day's a busy day. Jack wakes up at 6:00 A.M. and washes his face in a bowl of cold water. Then he hurries into a shirt and breeches, a kind of pants that boys and men wore. Before breakfast, Jack carries water and firewood to the kitchen. This is a separate building behind his house. Then Jack gobbles up his hoecakes, or baked cornmeal cakes.

45

Daily Chores

Jack has lots of chores to do! Every day he helps in his father's shoemaking shop. In the morning, Jack delivers a pair of shoes to a customer. Then he goes to Market Square to buy eggs and potatoes. Sometimes, Jack stops at the printer's shop to buy a newspaper called the <u>Virginia Gazette</u>. Jack feels proud that he helps his family.

School at Home

Jack loves to learn new things. There are no schools in Williamsburg. But Jack's father teaches him at home to read, write, and solve simple math problems. When Jack turns 12, he will become his father's **apprentice**, or helper, and learn to be a shoemaker.

47

Fun With a Friend

Jack likes to have fun, too. He goes hunting for wild grapes with his friend Jeremiah. Jack and his friend are very happy when they can play together.

The boys like to fish and swim in a nearby pond. Or they play a game of marbles. Sometimes they run next to a hoop, using a stick to balance it. Then it's time for evening chores.

The End of a Busy Day

After supper, Jack reads aloud to his mother, father, and sister. Then Jack's family shares stories and sings songs. Sometimes, Jack plays his tin whistle for everyone. Jack's busy day ends at about 8:00 P.M., when he goes upstairs to bed.

SHOW WHAT YOU KNOW!

THINK AND WRITE ABOUT IT

Put yourself in Jack's shoes in colonial times. Make a things-to-do list of your daily activities, beginning at 6:00 A.M. and ending at 8:00 P.M. Be sure to include your chores, meals, and school and home activities.

3

Key Word
independence

Greetings From San Antonio

• San Antonio, Texas

N W E S

Dear School Friends,

Hi! Welcome to San Antonio, Texas. My city has many exciting places to visit. These places tell the story of San Antonio's history from long ago to today. I am proud of my city. Did you know that many people here speak two languages? I can speak both English and Spanish. Maybe when I send my next postcard, I will greet you in Spanish!

Your Texas friend,

Diana

San Antonio
JAN. 18,
1996
U.S. Postal S

To: School Friends
Your School
Anytown, USA 00001

¡Buenos días!

This is the Alamo! In 1836, Texas was part of Mexico. But the people of Texas wanted their **independence**. They did not want to be part of Mexico. So Davy Crockett and a small group of Texans fought at the Alamo to be free. This battle helped to win independence for all Texans. We remember the Alamo and our heroes during Texas's Independence Day, in March, and the April Fiesta.

Your Texas amiga,

Diana

To: School Friends
Your School
Anytown, USA 00001

Davy Crockett ▶

Hello Friends,

   We are now at River Walk, a beautiful and fun place to visit in my city. But many years ago, it wasn't beautiful. The San Antonio River was full of garbage, so people cleaned it up. Now families come to concerts and ride in boats on the river. I love to watch the dancers at the Arneson River Theatre. When I grow up, I want to dance and wear colorful costumes, too!

                    Your friend,
                    Diana

San Antonio
JUNE 29
1996
U.S. Postal Service

To: School Friends
    Your School
    Anytown, USA 00001

¡Hola!

Hello! We're at the Institute of Texan Cultures. This is a fun place because you can touch some of the objects here. If you visit the museum in August, you can be part of the Texas Folklife Festival. This festival celebrates people from different cultures who live in Texas. This year I made an Indian hand drum, cooked a hoecake, watched a Polish dance, and listened to Scottish pipers. I can't wait until next year's festival!

Your school friend,

Diana

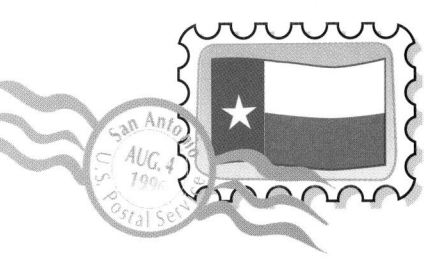

To: School Friends
Your School
Anytown, USA 00001

SHOW WHAT YOU KNOW!

THINK AND WRITE ABOUT IT

If you could visit one place in San Antonio, which place would it be? Why did you choose that place? What could you do there?

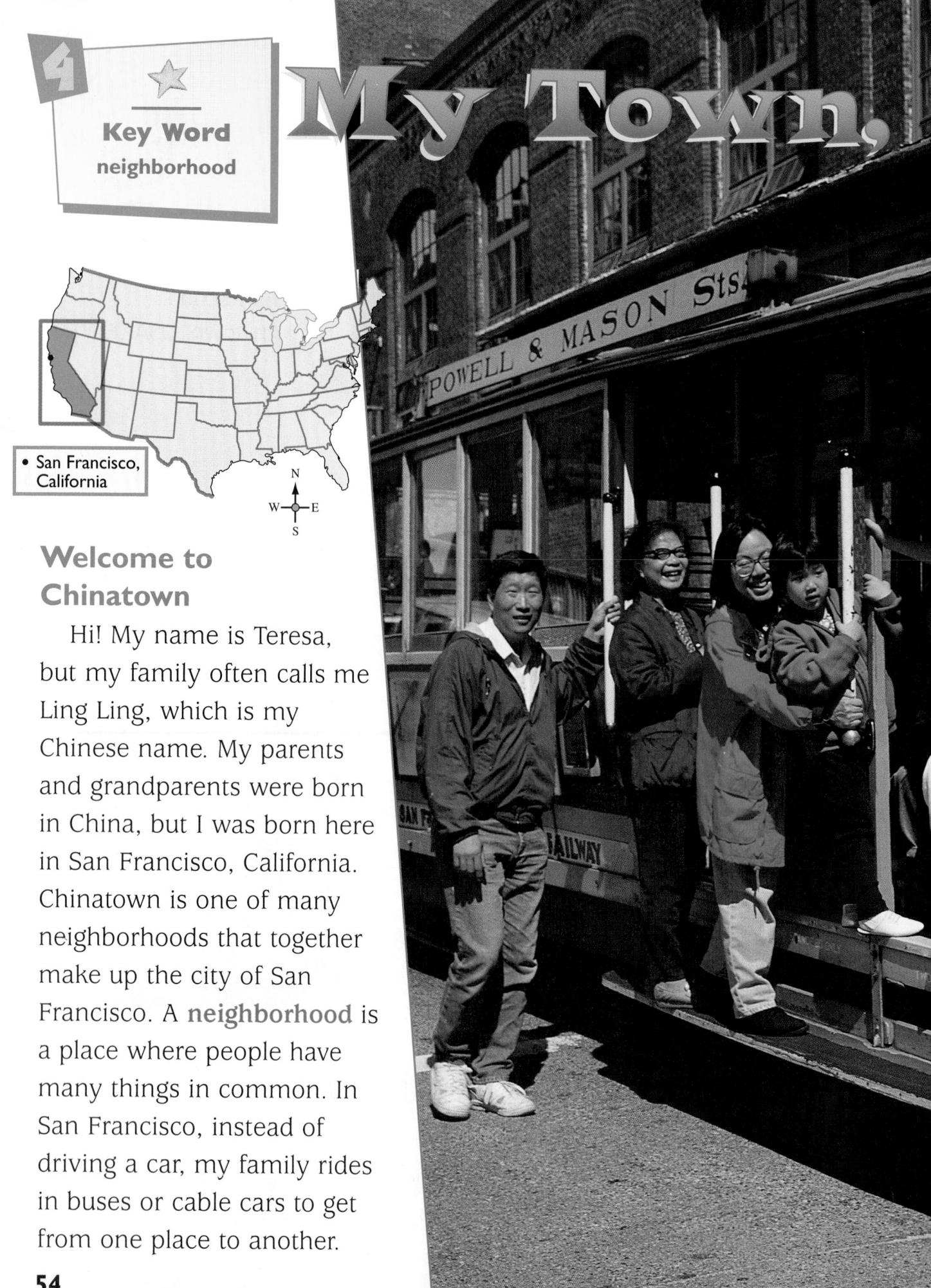

Key Word

neighborhood

• San Francisco, California

N
W E
S

Welcome to Chinatown

Hi! My name is Teresa, but my family often calls me Ling Ling, which is my Chinese name. My parents and grandparents were born in China, but I was born here in San Francisco, California. Chinatown is one of many neighborhoods that together make up the city of San Francisco. A **neighborhood** is a place where people have many things in common. In San Francisco, instead of driving a car, my family rides in buses or cable cars to get from one place to another.

54

Chinatown

Learning Two Languages

I can read both Chinese and English. So it's fun for me to walk around Chinatown because the shop and street signs are written in both languages. I also go to two schools. I go to a public school during the week. But on the weekends, I go to my Chinese school, where I speak Chinese.

I am also learning to write in Chinese. Chinese writing looks different from English words. I like writing in Chinese. It's like drawing pictures.

中國土成

▲ This is Teresa's Chinese writing. It means "Chinatown."

Let's Fly a Kite!

Many people come to Chinatown to visit. My favorite place is the kite shop. Another place I like is the park. When I am there, I often stop to watch people do tai chi. It looks like slow-motion exercise. Sometimes I watch my grandparents do tai chi. It's an exercise that keeps people healthy.

Sharing Chinese Customs

My family celebrates special holidays. My favorite is Chinese New Year. It is a custom to give oranges as presents. Another custom is to dress in special clothes. San Francisco has the largest Chinese New Year celebration in the United States. People from all of San Francisco's neighborhoods come to watch the big parade.

I like to visit other neighborhoods, too. My family and I go to North Beach for pizza. I like living in San Francisco because there are many neighborhoods with people from all over the world living in them. Do you live in a neighborhood within a city?

MAP ADVENTURE

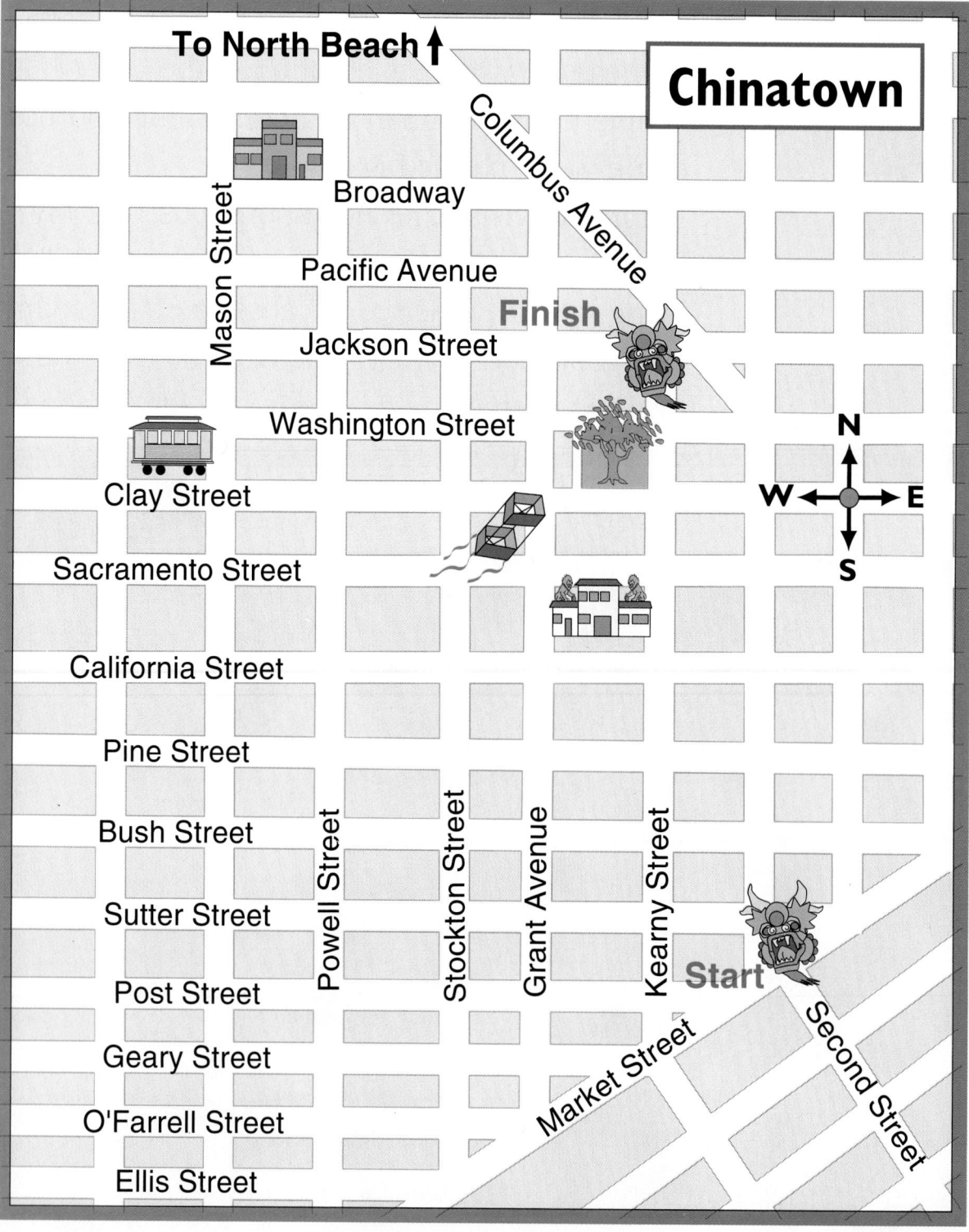

To North Beach ↑

Chinatown

Columbus Avenue

Broadway

Pacific Avenue

Finish

Jackson Street

Washington Street

Clay Street

Sacramento Street

California Street

Pine Street

Bush Street

Sutter Street

Post Street

Geary Street

O'Farrell Street

Ellis Street

Mason Street

Powell Street

Stockton Street

Grant Avenue

Kearny Street

N
W E
S

Start

Market Street

Second Street

Getting Around Chinatown

The map shows the locations of places you read about. Find these places. The map key will help you.

Chinatown Map Key

 Cable car stop

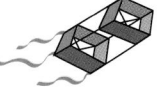 Kite shop

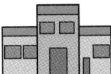 Teresa's public school

 Park

 Teresa's Chinese school

 Chinese New Year parade

SHOW WHAT YOU KNOW!

MAP IT

Read the directions below for the Chinese New Year parade. Then on the map trace the route, or path, with your finger.

- Start at the corner of Second Street and Market Street.
- Go south and west on Market Street.
- Turn north onto Stockton Street.
- Turn east onto Post Street.
- Turn north onto Kearny Street.
- Go north on Kearny Street until you are past Jackson Street.

EXPLORE IT

If you could make up a different parade route, what would it be? Think of a route and trace it.

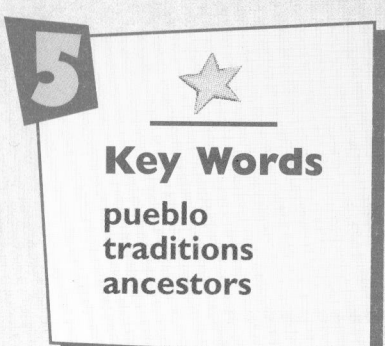

5

Key Words

pueblo
traditions
ancestors

Growing Up in a
Pueblo Community

• Taos, New Mexico

Sharing Traditions

Meet Tony, a Native American boy who lives in Taos, New Mexico. Tony's community is called the Taos Pueblo. **Pueblo** means "town." Tony, his family, and the people in his community share many **traditions** that are important to them. Traditions are things that are done certain ways for many years. Step inside Tony's world as he learns about these traditions.

A Tradition of Song

Tony hears the beat of the deer-hide drum. Great-grandfather sings songs from long ago. He sings in their Tiwa language. Songs are passed down from the pueblo's elders.

The words are not written down. Tony listens. The songs teach him how to respect nature. When Tony becomes a man, he will beat the drum and sing these same songs to his children.

A Tradition of Dance

Tony dances to say thanks. He wears feathers of hawks, bones of deer, and quills of porcupines. He dances his thanks for the gifts of the earth. He dances to make seasons change and plants grow. He dances as his **ancestors** danced long ago. The feathers he wears spread as he gives thanks. Tony has been learning traditional dances since he was four years old.

A Tasty Tradition

After school, Tony rides his bike in the pueblo. He visits his grandmother. She takes the bread from a horno, or oven. After the wood fire burns out, she removes the ashes. Then she puts more dough in to make more bread. A horno holds heat even when there is no fire. The bread bakes in the horno. On his way home, Tony eats some of the fresh warm bread.

SHOW WHAT YOU KNOW!

THINK AND WRITE ABOUT IT

Think of a family tradition of your own. Then write about it and explain why it is a tradition.

6

Key Words
freedom
colonies
document

Let's Celebrate Our History!

Celebrating Holidays

Everybody loves holidays. Sometimes they are so much fun that we forget why we celebrate them. Many holidays celebrate our country's history. They remind us of why our country is special. One of the reasons is that it is a place where everyone can work, play, and live in **freedom**. Freedom allows people to choose how they want to live. So join us as we celebrate our one big community—the United States of America!

▲ "The First Thanksgiving at Plymouth, Massachusetts" by Jennie Brownscombe

Thanksgiving Then

Do you know why we celebrate Thanksgiving? About 400 years ago, people called Pilgrims left the country of England. They wanted to live where they could choose their own religion. So they set sail for this country on a ship called the <u>Mayflower</u>. They called their new community Plymouth.

The first winter was very cold, and the Pilgrims did not have enough to eat. Native Americans helped them grow food. The Pilgrims invited them to a harvest feast. On this day the Pilgrims gave thanks to God. This day was our country's first Thanksgiving, a holiday we celebrate today.

Thanksgiving Now

Today, many people in the United States celebrate Thanksgiving with their families and friends on the fourth Thursday of November. It is a time to give thanks for our food, clothing, and homes. People show their thanks in many ways. Some show thanks by helping other people in their communities. How do you celebrate this holiday?

Independence Day Then

After the Pilgrims came to this country, many more people came. They lived in 13 **colonies**, or places that are ruled by a country far away. These colonies were ruled by an English king.

The king had many rules and laws for the colonists to obey. But the colonists didn't think these laws were fair. So they wrote a **document** called the Declaration of Independence. It said that all people have a right to be free. But the king didn't agree, and the War of Independence began. In the end the colonists won! We remember July 4, 1776, because this was the day that the colonies declared their independence from England.

Independence Day Now

Today, Independence Day, also known as the Fourth of July, is our country's biggest summer holiday. Many families have picnics. Many communities have fireworks. And people of all ages march in parades to celebrate our freedom. Others give speeches and tell stories about our country and why it is a great place to live. How do you celebrate Independence Day?

Dr. Martin Luther King, Jr.

As a boy, Martin Luther King, Jr., liked to do some of the same things that you like to do. He sang, played baseball, and flew his kite.

Many black people were treated unfairly. In some places they were forced to sit at the backs of buses and drink at separate water fountains. When Martin grew up, he decided to fight for the rights of all people. He wanted all people to be treated the same.

Instead of using his fists to fight, Dr. King used his words. In a famous speech, he shared his dream that one day all people would respect each other.

He and others, including young people, marched peacefully in support of his dream. Although he was killed in 1968, many people share his dream today.

Martin Luther King, Jr. Day

Each year we remember Dr. King on January 15, his birthday. Like the colonists who signed the Declaration of Independence and the Pilgrims from Plymouth, Dr. King believed that all people have the right to be free. So on Dr. King's birthday, Independence Day, and Thanksgiving, we remember our country's history. And we celebrate our one great community—the United States of America.

SHOW WHAT YOU KNOW!

THINK ABOUT IT AND DRAW IT

Make a quilt square that shows something that you can do because you are free. Put everyone's squares together to make a freedom quilt.

SUMMING UP

1 DO YOU REMEMBER...

1. What are some ways Kim has changed since she was a baby?

2. Describe a day in the life of a boy in colonial times.

3. If your friend was taking a trip to San Antonio, what could you say about one of the exciting places to visit in this city?

4. Describe a Chinese New Year custom of Teresa's.

5. How does Tony learn about his ancestors and pueblo life from long ago?

6. Why did the Pilgrims, colonists, and Dr. King each want freedom for themselves and other people?

2 USING YOUR SKILLS

Use the Venn diagram below to show how you and one of the children you read about are both alike and different. First, choose a child. Then copy the diagram. Now add your ideas to it.

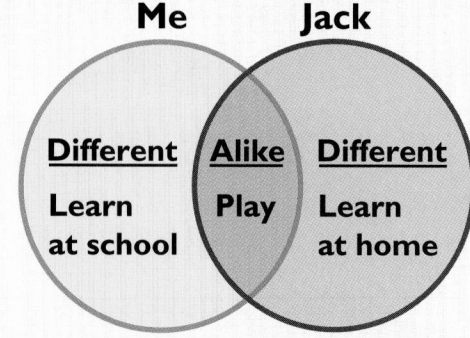

Me   **Jack**

Different   **Alike**   **Different**

Learn   Play   Learn
at school   at home

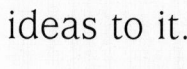

3 WHAT DO YOU THINK?

1. Name five ways you've changed since kindergarten.

2. How is your life different from Jack's?

3. If you could visit one of the places you read about, where would you go? Why?

4. Why are traditions important?

4 USING YOUR WORDS

Use the word next to each child's name in a sentence that tells something about the child. Remember to write complete sentences.

Kim	change
Jack	apprentice
Diana	independence
Teresa	neighborhood
Tony	traditions

5 YOU CAN READ MAPS

This map shows where each of the children you read about lives. Find the locations of these places. Then answer the questions.

1. Who lives the farthest from Kim?

2. Who lives the closest to Jack?

3. Who lives the farthest from Tony?

4. Which two children live in neighboring states?

5. Which two children live the farthest apart?

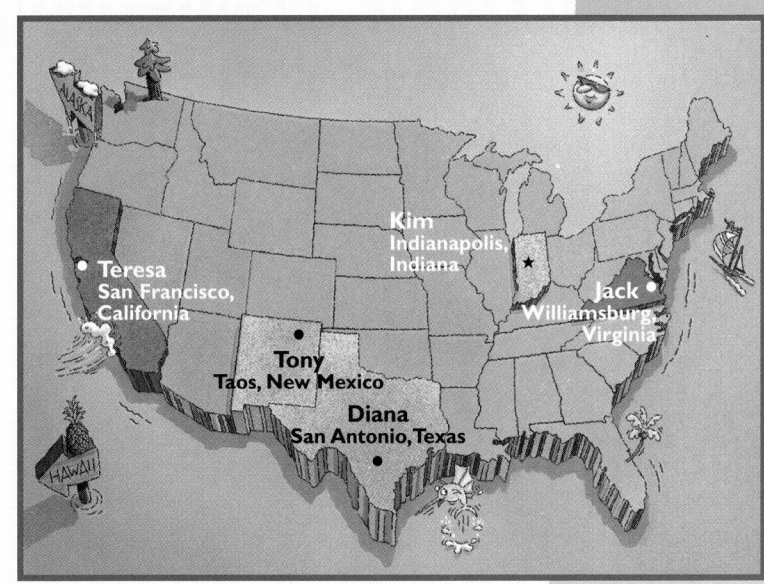

The Environment

Every Day Is Earth Day

Save a forest, plant a tree,
Turn out lights, save energy.
An elephant and a panda bear
Need our help, concern, and care.
Look at what you throw away,
Recycle paper every day.
Show you care in every way
By having Earth Day every day!

The Environment

The earth is home to all living things. It's up to us to keep it a clean and safe place for everyone and everything.

CONTENTS

▼ What is this girl holding? Find out on page 85.

These books are about the importance of keeping the earth clean and safe for all living things. Read one that interests you and fill out a book-review form.

READ AND FIND OUT

It's My Earth, Too: How I Can Help the Earth Stay Alive by **Kathleen Krull, illustrated by Melanie Hope Greenberg** (Bantam Doubleday Dell Publishing Group, 1992)
The earth has many gifts to give us. Read about 12 ways you can help keep our earth alive.

Earth Day by **Linda Lowery, illustrations by Mary Bergherr** (Carolrhoda Books, 1991)
Read about our country's first Earth Day celebration. Then learn how Earth Day came to be celebrated around the world and how you can be a part of it.

Hey! Get Off Our Train by **John Burningham** (Crown Publishing Group, 1994)
Find out why animals from around the world want to board a boy's nighttime toy train.

Sharing the Earth

Welcome to Our Home!

Did you know that people, plants, and animals share one big home called the **earth**? It is where we get the **natural resources** we need to live. These natural resources include air to breathe, water to drink, and land to grow food.

It is our responsibility to care for our home, the earth. We also need to use our natural resources wisely.

Caring for Our Air

When you look up into the sky, what do you see? The sky is blue when the air is clean. But when the air is dirty, the sky can look brown. People and animals need air to breathe. Air is also important to trees and other plants. Unclean air can hurt them.

Cars, buses, planes, and trains can put unhealthy gases into the air. So the next time you think you need a car to get somewhere, see if you can walk or ride your bike instead. Or maybe you can car pool, or share a ride with friends.

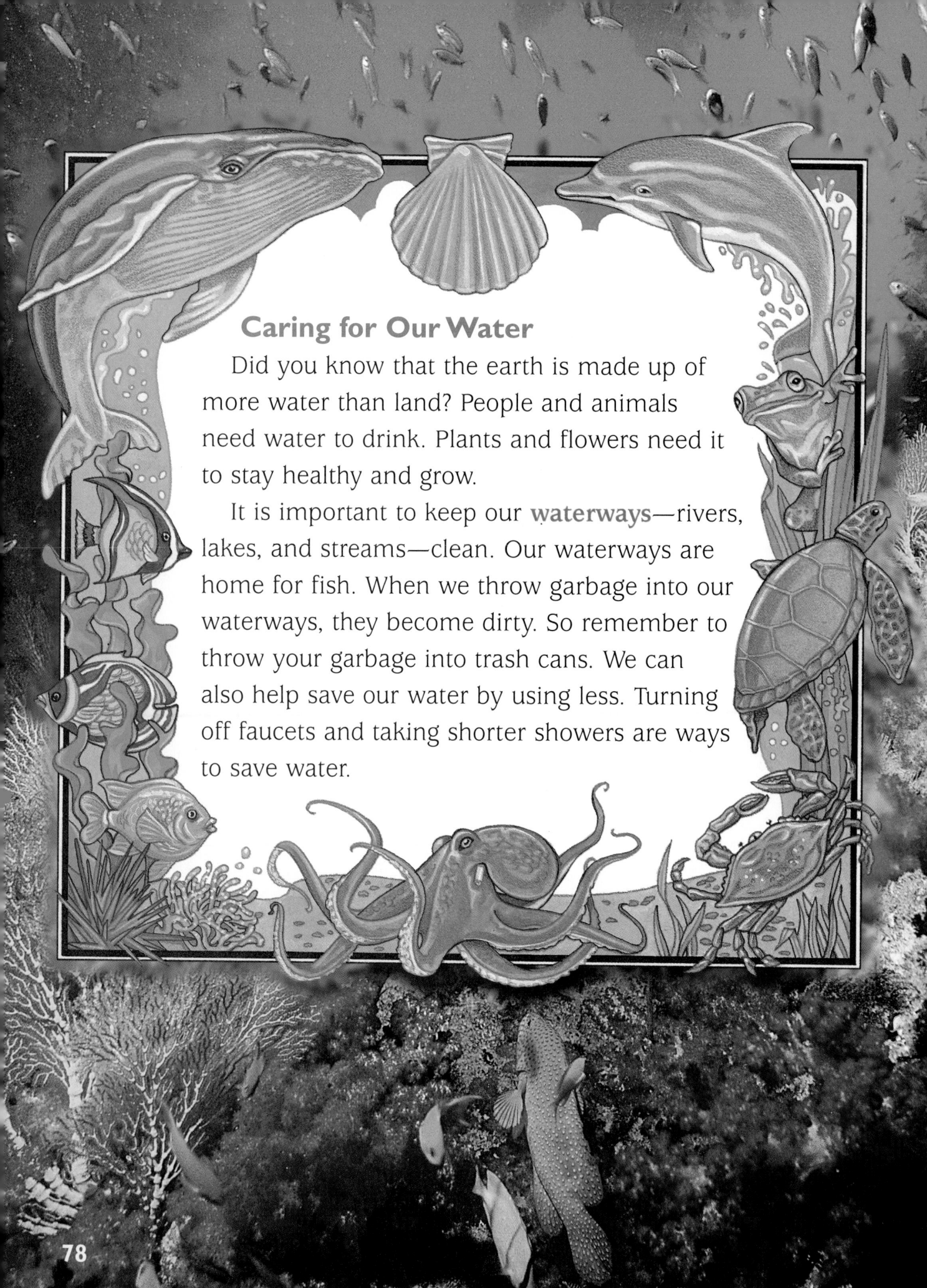

Caring for Our Water

Did you know that the earth is made up of more water than land? People and animals need water to drink. Plants and flowers need it to stay healthy and grow.

It is important to keep our waterways—rivers, lakes, and streams—clean. Our waterways are home for fish. When we throw garbage into our waterways, they become dirty. So remember to throw your garbage into trash cans. We can also help save our water by using less. Turning off faucets and taking shorter showers are ways to save water.

Caring for Our Land

Think about biting into a tasty apple or munching on a carrot stick. These foods and many others are grown on the earth's land. Our land is made up of rich soil. We need healthy soil and clean air and water to grow our food.

Now it's your turn. Plant some seeds. Water the soil. Then watch and enjoy what you grow.

SHOW WHAT YOU KNOW!

THINK ABOUT IT AND DRAW IT

Think of ways you can care for the earth's air, water, and land. Draw and label a picture of each.

2

Key Words
environments
rain forest

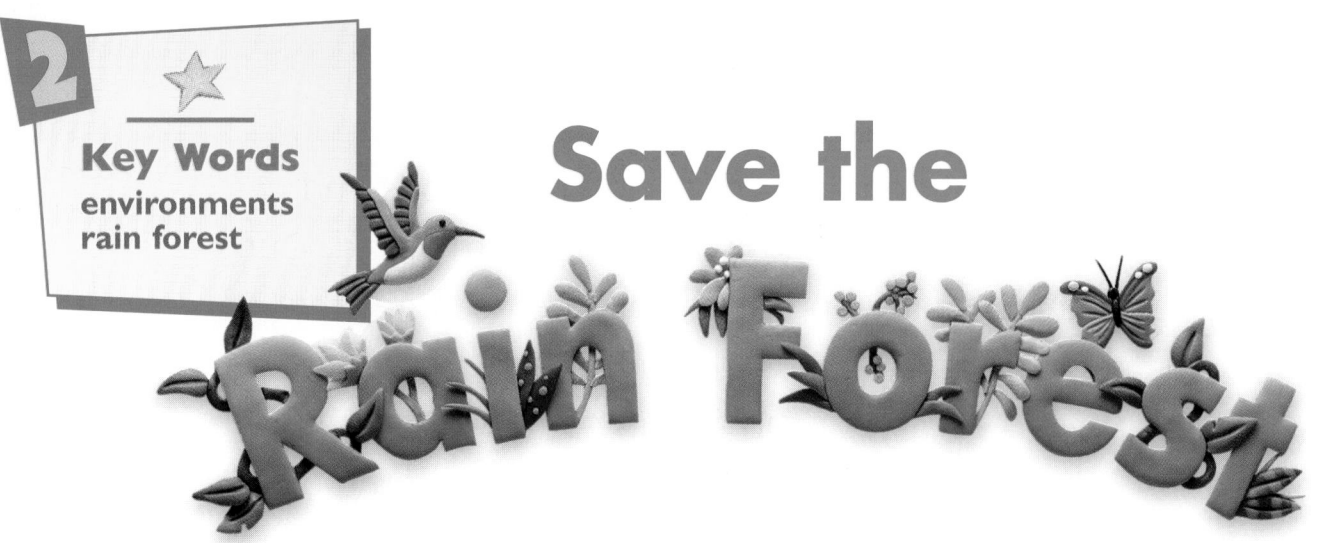

Save the Rain Forest

A Rain Forest Environment

The earth is home to many **environments**. Some environments, such as deserts, are dry and hot. Another environment, called a tropical **rain forest**, is very wet and warm. In fact, it rains more than 200 days a year in a rain forest.

Rain forests are home to half of our earth's treasures—animals, birds, butterflies, insects, trees, and plants. They depend on the rain forests to live. The map shows where many of the earth's rain forests are located.

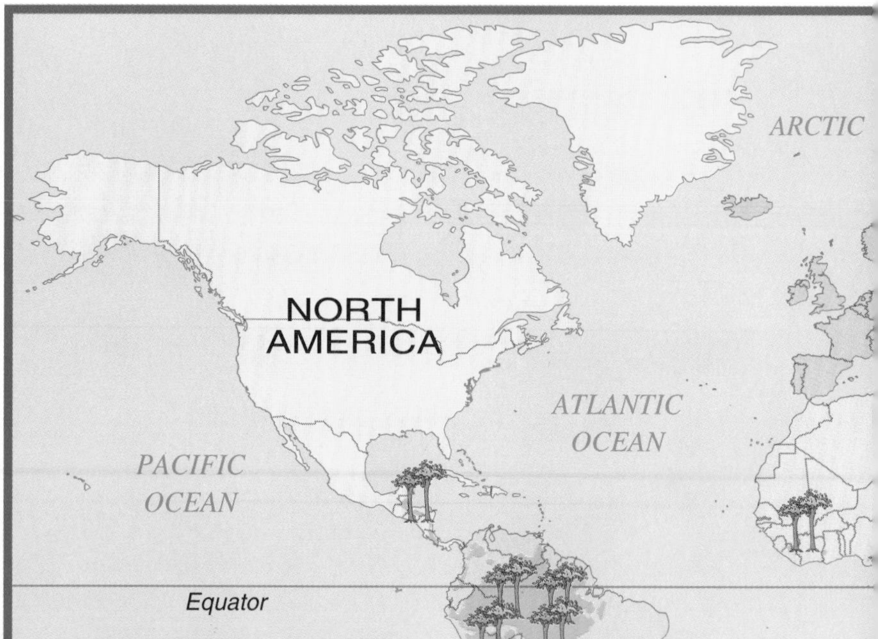

ARCTIC
NORTH AMERICA
ATLANTIC OCEAN
PACIFIC OCEAN
Equator
SOUTH AMERICA
ATLANTIC OCEAN
Rain Forests Around the World
Rain forest

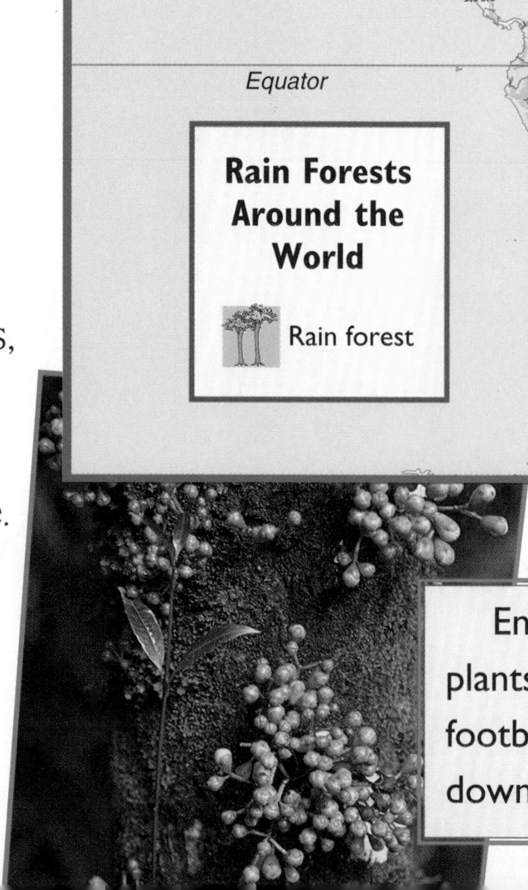

Enough trees and plants to cover 200 football fields are cut down every minute.

By the year 2035, there may not be any rain forests for animals to live in.

One third of all the birds in the world call a rain forest home.

Protecting Rain Forests

Today, rain forests are being cut down to make room for farms and roads. Beautiful and useful plants and flowers have been destroyed. Many birds and animals no longer have homes.

Groups of people are trying to save the rain forests. There are now places where there is a limit to how many trees can be cut down. Let's explore a rain forest.

OCEAN

EUROPE

ASIA

PACIFIC OCEAN

AFRICA

Equator

INDIAN OCEAN

AUSTRALIA

N
W   E
S

ANTARCTICA

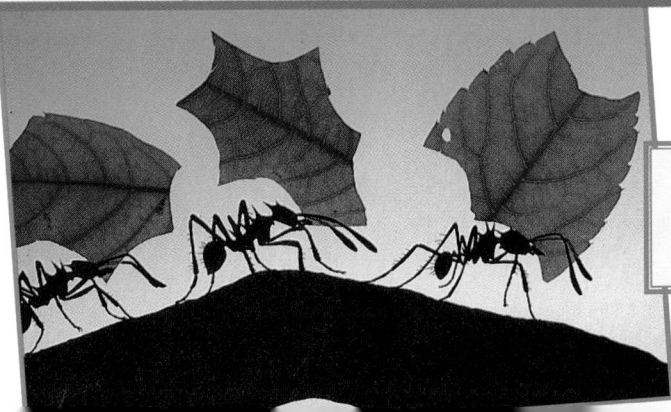

There are 30 to 80 million insects living in rain forests.

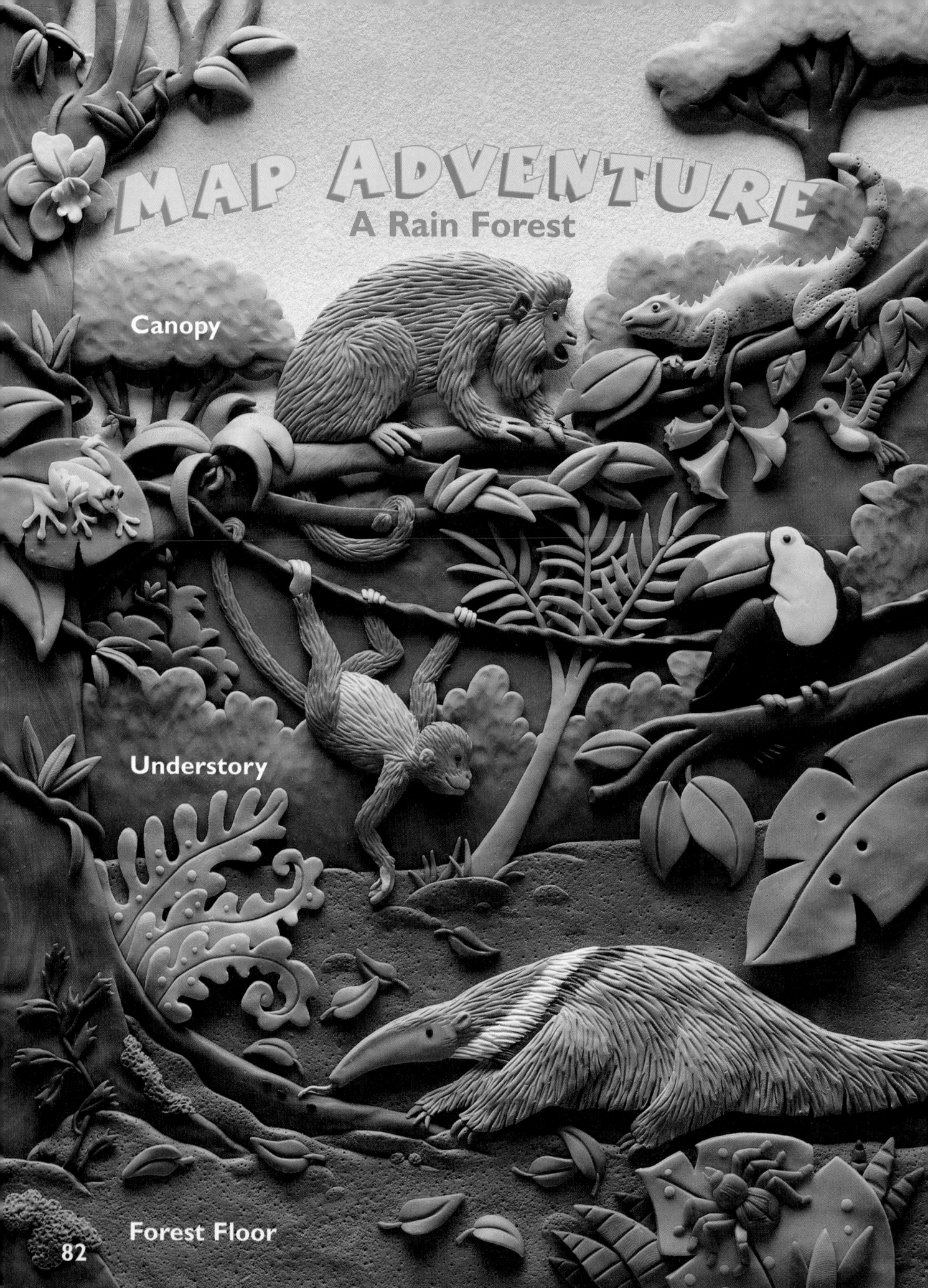

MAP ADVENTURE
A Rain Forest

Canopy

Understory

Forest Floor

Discovering a Rain Forest

Like a three-story house, a rain forest has three stories, called layers. First, vines grow on the forest floor, or bottom layer. Next, they grow through the understory, or middle layer. Finally, they grow to the canopy, or top layer.

Rain Forest Map Key

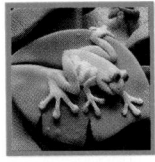 **Tree frog**

 **Howler monkey**

 **Toucan**

 **Spider monkey**

 **Hummingbird**

 **Herbs**

 **Tarantula**

 **Anteater**

SHOW WHAT YOU KNOW!

MAP IT

The map key shows some of the living things in a rain forest. The map shows which layer each lives in. Look at the map and tell where each plant or animal lives.

EXPLORE IT

Choose an animal or plant. Write why you think it lives in the rain forest layer that it does.

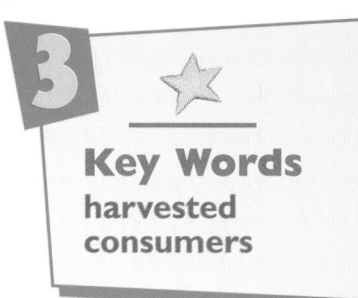

How We Get Cereal

From Tiny Plants to Cornflakes

Good morning! All across the United States, many people start their day by eating a bowl of cereal. Do you remember learning in Lesson 1 that the earth's soil helps us grow the food we need? Let's look at the steps it takes to make cornflakes—from tiny plants to a breakfast cereal.

Corn is planted on farms in early spring. On the United States map below, you can see where most corn grows.

Where the Most Corn Grows

☐ Corn

Harvesting Time

In the fall the corn on the cob is **harvested**, or gathered. Most farmers harvest corn by using large machines. The machines remove tiny pieces, called kernels, from the corncobs. Trucks take the kernels to buildings where the kernels are dried. Then the kernels are moved by truck or train to a mill.

From Grits to Cornflakes

A mill grinds the kernels into grits. The grits are taken to cereal companies. There the grits are cooked, pressed, dried, and toasted to make cornflakes. Then the cornflakes are put into boxes and shipped to warehouses.

From Warehouse to Cereal Bowl

Finally, supermarkets buy the boxes of cornflakes and sell them to **consumers**, or people who buy food and other goods. The next time you have cornflakes, remember that it's a long trip from a cornfield to your cereal bowl. Then eat up and enjoy!

SHOW WHAT YOU KNOW!

THINK AND WRITE ABOUT IT

Listed below are four of the steps in making cereal. Write the steps in the order in which they happen.

- Cooking
- Grinding
- Planting
- Harvesting

4

Key Words
endangered
extinct

Our Friends

▲ Koala

Endangered Animals

In countries near and far, there are **endangered** animals who need our help. These animals are in danger of becoming **extinct**, or dying out. Meet three children—Mario from Brazil, Chanya from Kenya, and Cheng Fu from China. Their letters tell you about some animal friends in need. The map below shows where these animals live.

American bald eagle ▶

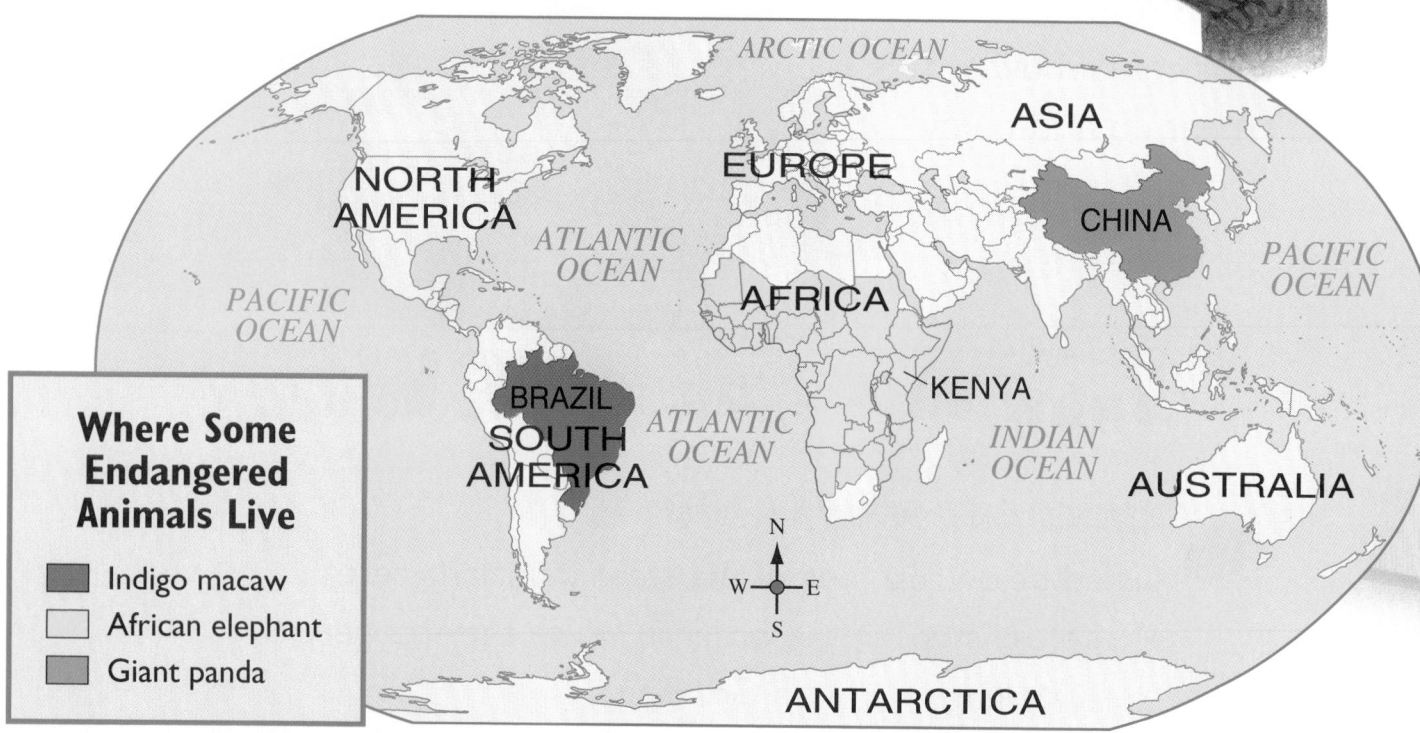

Where Some Endangered Animals Live

- Indigo macaw
- African elephant
- Giant panda

ARCTIC OCEAN

ASIA

EUROPE

NORTH AMERICA

CHINA

ATLANTIC OCEAN

PACIFIC OCEAN

PACIFIC OCEAN

AFRICA

BRAZIL
SOUTH AMERICA

KENYA

ATLANTIC OCEAN

INDIAN OCEAN

AUSTRALIA

N
W · E
S

ANTARCTICA

in **N**eed

Dear Friends,

Indigo macaws are large parrots found in Brazil. That's where I live.

Indigo macaws are smart because they can talk. But these birds are in danger. They need to eat the nuts from palm trees. But farmers are cutting down palm trees to make room for other animals. The macaws are starving. My country is trying to protect these endangered birds. There are now places for the macaws to live where trees cannot be cut down.

Yesterday I found a macaw's feather. I'm keeping it in my journal to remember my bird friends.

Sincerely,
Mario

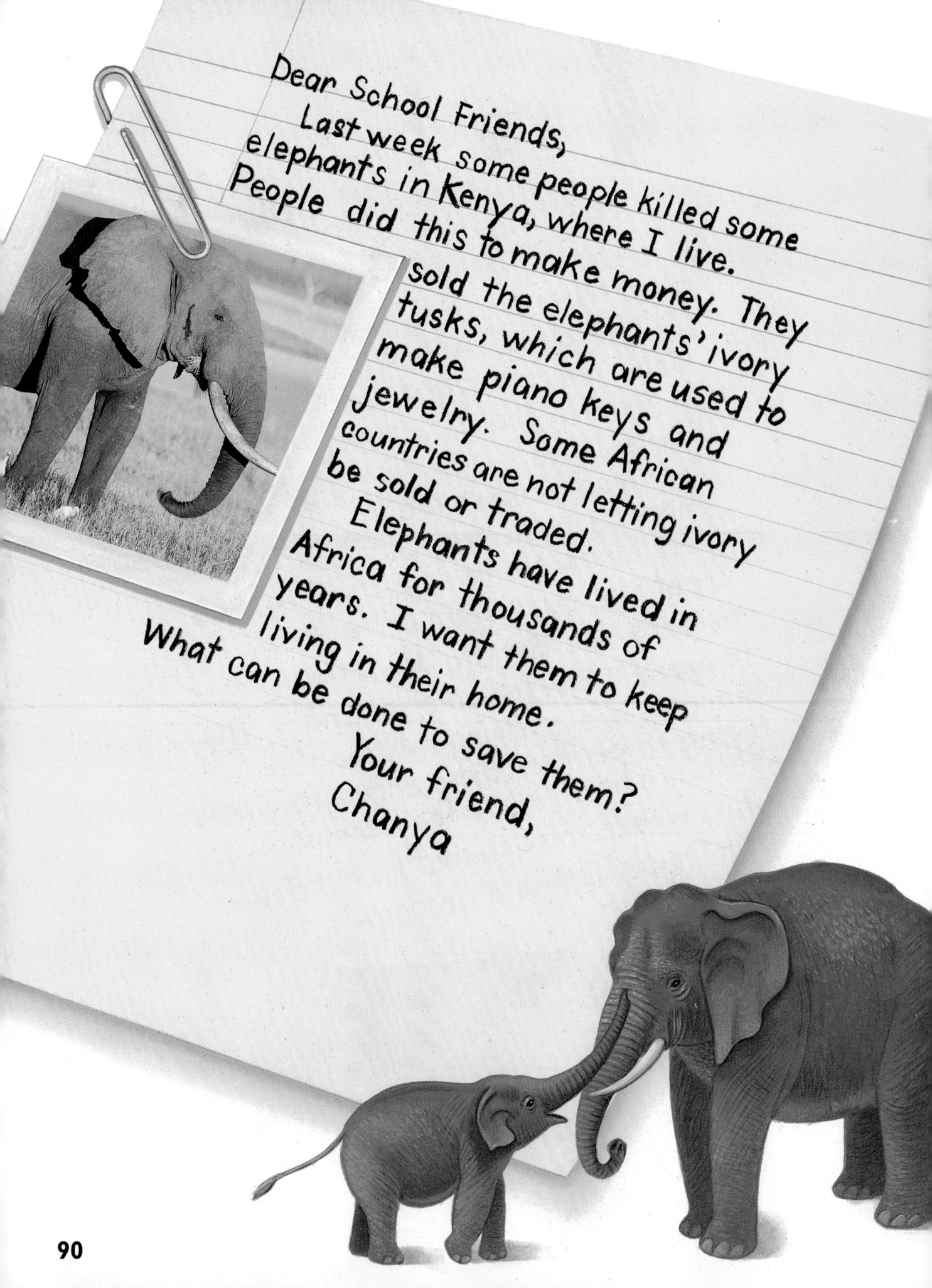

Dear School Friends,

Last week some people killed some elephants in Kenya, where I live. People did this to make money. They sold the elephants' ivory tusks, which are used to make piano keys and jewelry. Some African countries are not letting ivory be sold or traded.

Elephants have lived in Africa for thousands of years. I want them to keep living in their home. What can be done to save them?

Your friend,
Chanya

Dear Friends,
   I am sending you sad news from China. My animal friends, the giant pandas, are starving. Their home in the bamboo forest is being cut down to make room for farms. The pandas need to eat bamboo every day, and now there isn't enough of it.
   My country is helping them by setting up feeding stations and planting more bamboo. Can you think of another way to help our pandas?
                          Sincerely,
                          Cheng Fu

SHOW WHAT YOU KNOW!

DRAW IT AND WRITE ABOUT IT

On a piece of paper, draw a picture of an endangered animal you read about. Then write where it lives, what is happening to it, and how you can help it.

5

Key Words
reduce
reuse
recycle

Let's Clean Up!

Cleaning Up Our Waterways

All around the world, people are working side by side to save the earth. In many parts of the world, people have cleaned up thousands of miles of beaches and waterways. These waterways include rivers, lakes, and streams.

Each year, many children and adults help to collect more than 4 million pounds of trash. Some of this trash is used to make new things, such as glass bottles.

Citizens Clean Up

The cleanup effort began in 1986 in Texas. Citizens collected trash along the beaches by the Gulf of Mexico. Since then many states have a yearly cleanup day. One of the most successful is in North Carolina. Every September, thousands of volunteers collect trash. Have you ever thought about why it's so important to keep our beaches and waterways clean?

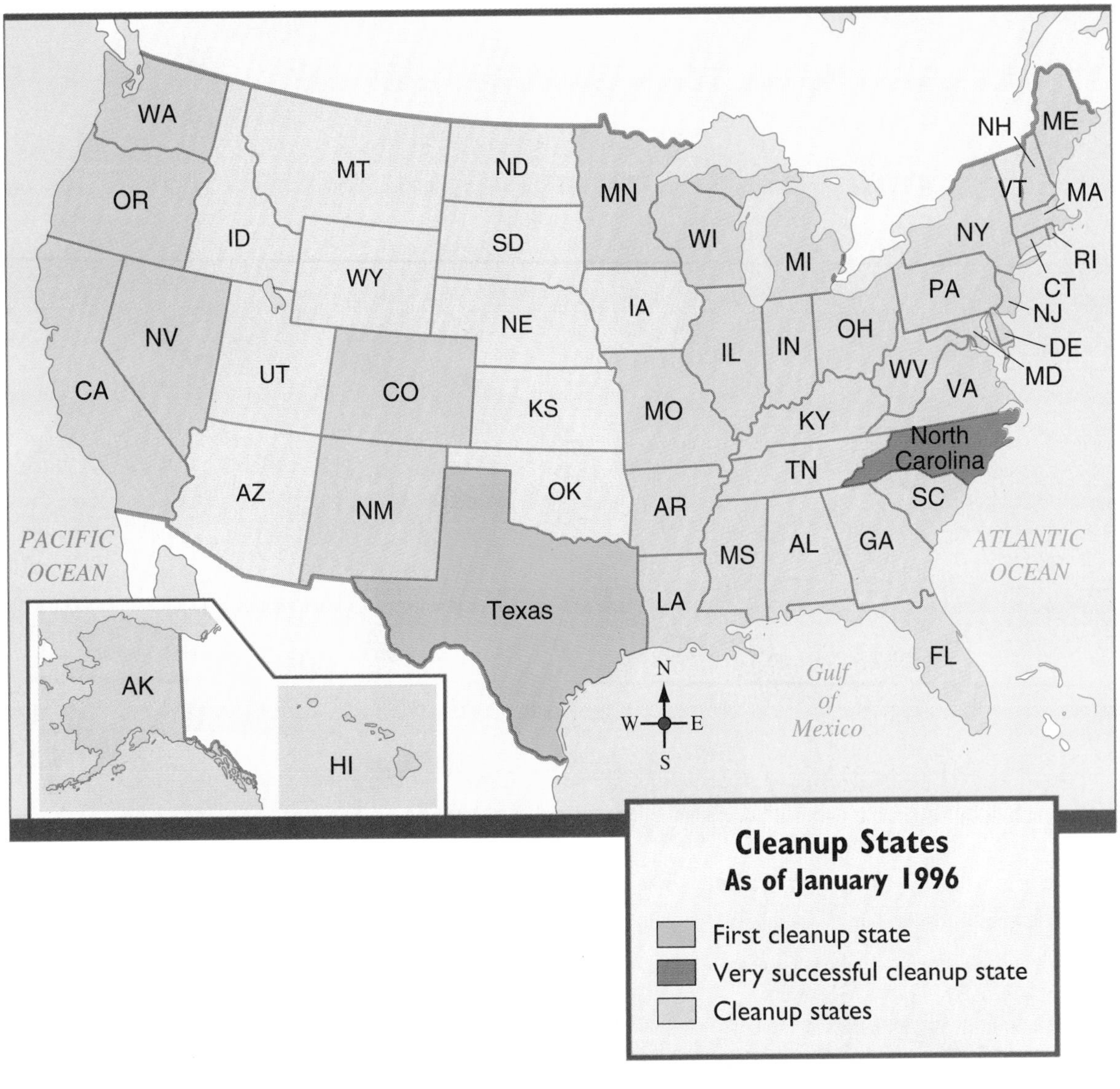

Cleanup States
As of January 1996

- First cleanup state
- Very successful cleanup state
- Cleanup states

Caring for Animals

Citizens have found televisions, chairs, money, clothing, and even toothbrushes when cleaning up.

Many of these materials harm animals. Birds can get their beaks caught on six-pack rings. Whales and turtles mistake plastic for food and eat it. Then they don't have room left for real food, and they can starve.

Trash can even hurt people. We can cut our feet on broken glass left on beaches.

Reduce, Reuse, and Recycle

Look around where you live and go to school. You can **reduce** the amount of paper you use by writing on the back of each sheet. Bring food to school in a lunch box rather than in a paper bag.

Reuse plastic cups and spoons by washing them and using them again. **Recycle** glass, paper, and plastic so that new glass, paper, and plastic products can be made. Can you think of other things you can reduce, reuse, and recycle?

What Our Class Recycles in a Week

	25 pieces of paper
	16 glass bottles
	10 tin cans
	6 plastic bottles
	4 magazines

SHOW WHAT YOU KNOW!

THINK AND WRITE ABOUT IT

Be a good citizen! In a journal, keep track of how you reduce, reuse, and recycle daily.

Key Words
polluted
senator

It's Earth Day Every Day!

A Special Day of the Year

Every year on April 22, something very special happens. People around the world share one common concern—the earth's need for our help and care.

April 22 is Earth Day. On this day, we learn about endangered animals and **polluted**, or unclean, air. We also work together to help solve these and other problems. Earth Day is a day to take responsibility for cleaning up our home—together.

It's Our Responsibility

Earth Day was begun more than 25 years ago by a **senator**, or lawmaker, from Wisconsin. Senator Nelson thought that citizens of the United States should take more responsibility in caring for the earth's natural resources. He thought that people were careless with the land, air, water, plants, and animals.

Senator Nelson hoped that on Earth Day everyone would learn many ways to care for and respect the earth.

Learning and Working Together

On April 22, 1970, more than 20 million Americans took part in the first Earth Day. Across the country, people celebrated in many ways. Citizens took classes to learn about pollution and recycling. Some marched in parades. Others sang songs about the environment. And many people took nature walks and planted trees. In hundreds of ways, people showed their concern. Today the earth needs our help just as much as ever.

Earth Day Around the World

Earth Day is now celebrated in many countries around the world. Side by side, adults and children reduce, reuse, and recycle trash. They ride bikes instead of cars to lessen the amount of air pollution. They plant trees, paint murals, and celebrate the earth's beauty. And they give money to groups who help to save rain forests and endangered animals. You don't have to wait until April 22 to care. You can celebrate Earth Day every day!

SHOW WHAT YOU KNOW!

THINK ABOUT IT AND DRAW IT

Think about how you would like to celebrate Earth Day with your friends. Draw a picture of it. Then try it out.

SUMMING UP

1 DO YOU REMEMBER . . .

1. Name three important natural resources.

2. What are the three layers that make up a rain forest?

3. What are consumers?

4. What does the term "endangered animal" mean?

5. Name something you can do each day to reduce, reuse, and recycle.

6. Why was Earth Day started in 1970?

3 WHAT DO YOU THINK?

1. Take turns with a classmate telling about a natural resource that is needed to grow corn and other foods we eat. Then tell why the natural resource is needed.

2. If you were a giant panda from China and could talk, what would you ask people to do to help you?

3. What are some ways that one person could make a difference in caring for our waterways?

4. If you were president of an Earth Day celebration, what three activities would you have?

2 USING YOUR SKILLS

The table at right lists some of the steps in making cornflakes. On a separate sheet of paper, write the correct order in which the steps happen.

Steps in Making Cornflakes
• Corn is harvested, and the corn kernels are removed.
• Corn is planted on farms.
• A mill grinds the kernels into grits.
• The grits are cooked, pressed, dried, and toasted.
• The kernels are dried.
• The kernels are taken to a mill.

4 USING YOUR WORDS

If today was Earth Day and you were invited to make the opening speech to start the celebration, what would you say? Use at least five words from this list in your speech. Write what you would say. Then practice giving your speech to a friend.

consumers	harvested	reduce
earth	natural resources	reuse
endangered	polluted	senator
environments	rain forest	waterways
extinct	recycle	

5 YOU CAN READ MAPS

On this map, you can see where some of the endangered animals that need our help live. Look at the map and the map key. Then name each animal and the continent where it lives.

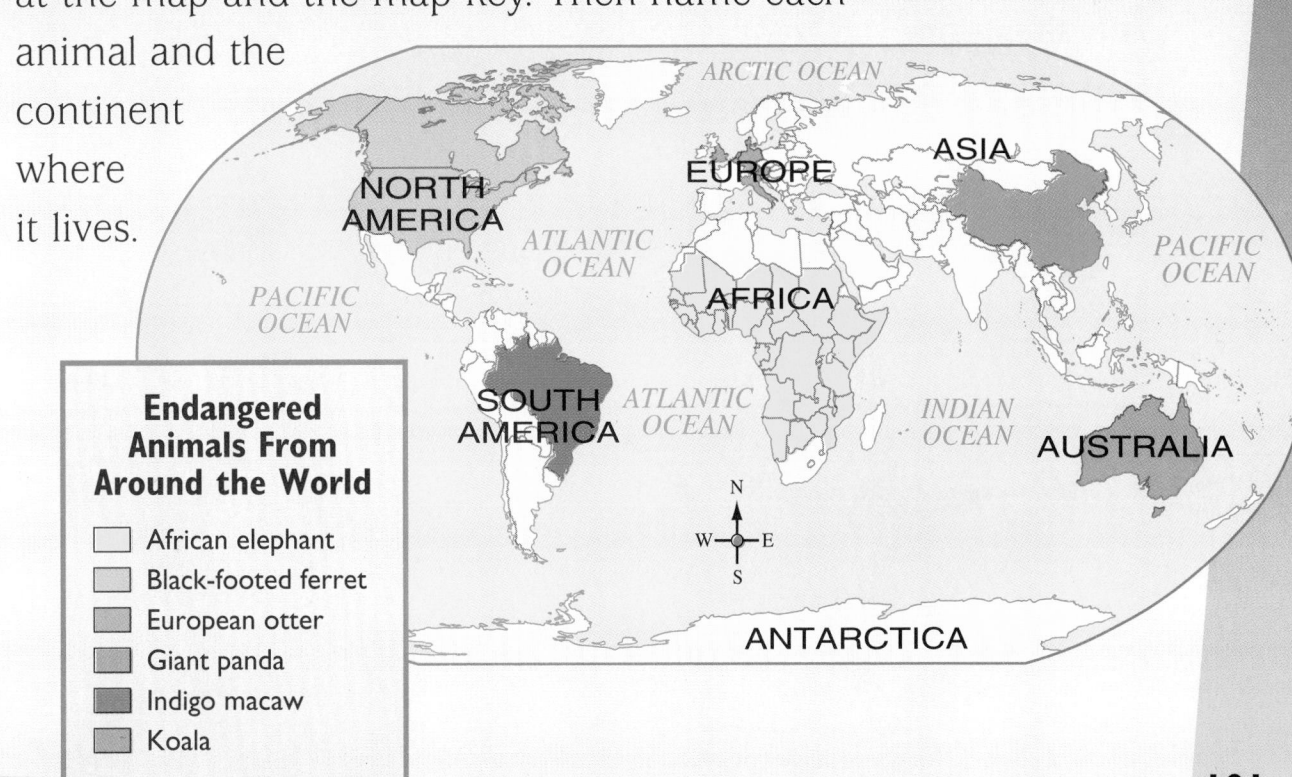

Endangered Animals From Around the World

- African elephant
- Black-footed ferret
- European otter
- Giant panda
- Indigo macaw
- Koala

101

ALL AROUND THE WORLD

CANADA

NORTH AMERICA

Montreal

UNITED STATES

• Jonesborough

Los Angeles

MEXICO

Hawaii

Mexico City

ATLANTIC OCEAN

PACIFIC OCEAN

SOUTH AMERICA

PERU

Pack your passport, maps, and gear,
It's time to travel far and near.
Visit sites along the way,
Your adventure starts today!

N

W   *E*

S

ARCTIC OCEAN

ASIA

EUROPE

GREECE

CHINA

EGYPT

AFRICA

THAILAND

PACIFIC
OCEAN

INDIAN
OCEAN

AUSTRALIA

Sydney

ATLANTIC
OCEAN

ANTARCTICA

Theme 4

All Around

▼ Where did this girl's basketball come from? Find out on page 123.

All aboard! Take a trip around the world to visit new places. See how people who live far away from each other can be alike.

CONTENTS

the World

These books tell about people and places from around the world. Read one that interests you and fill out a book-review form.

READ AND FIND OUT

A Is for Africa by Ifeoma Onyefulu
(Penguin USA, 1993)
Visit the friendly people of Africa. Look at the games the children play. Find out how their lives are both alike and different from yours.

My Wish for Tomorrow: Words and Pictures From Children Around the World by Jim Henson Publishing and the United Nations (William Morrow & Co., 1995)
The boys and girls of many countries share their wishes for our world. What wish do you have to make the world a better place?

How to Make an Apple Pie and See the World by Marjorie Priceman (Alfred A. Knopf, 1994)
Did you ever wonder where the sugar, flour, and cinnamon for an apple pie come from? Travel around the world to find out.

From City to City

A School Day in Montreal

Hi! My name is Marie. It's time to visit the city where I live, Montreal, Canada. Our first stop is my school. I go there from September to June. School begins at 9 A.M. and ends at 3 P.M.

My favorite subject is social studies. I also like to work on the computer. We learn French and English in our school because many Canadians speak both languages. "Parlez-vous Français?" Do you speak French?

During the winter I go ice skating with my friend. I also like to play ice hockey. This is a popular sport in Canada.

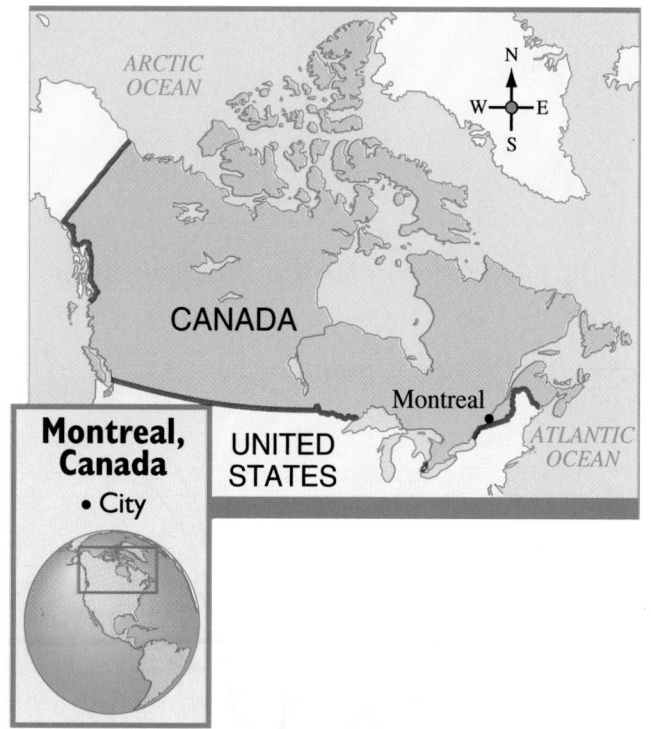

Montreal, Canada
• City

Canada Day

I live in an old part of Montreal. Some of the homes here are more than 200 years old. My stone house has a very steep roof so that the snow can slide down. It snows a lot in Montreal.

During the summer my family and I celebrate Canada Day. We honor the day that our country became independent from Great Britain—July 1, 1867. On Canada Day we watch singers and dancers perform, and we go to baseball games. We have a lot of fun. I hope you enjoyed your visit to Montreal. "Au revoir" and goodbye!

A School Day in Mexico City

Welcome! My name is Pedro. Come along with me to Mexico City, the **capital** of Mexico. A capital is a city or town where leaders of a country make laws. We speak Spanish in my country. Our first stop is my school. I go there from September to June. School begins at 8 A.M. and ends at 1 P.M. My favorite subjects are reading and music.

When I get home from school, my family and I sit down to a big meal. Then I do my homework. I like to play soccer with my brother after I've done my homework. Many people in Mexico enjoy playing and watching soccer.

Mexico City, Mexico

⊛ National capital

Mexican Independence Day

September 16 is a very important day in my country. On this day in 1810, Mexicans began their fight for freedom from Spain. Mexico won its independence in 1821.

My family and I enjoy celebrating Mexico's independence. We go to parades and ceremonies. We have a lot of fun. Have you enjoyed learning about life in my country? "Adios" and goodbye!

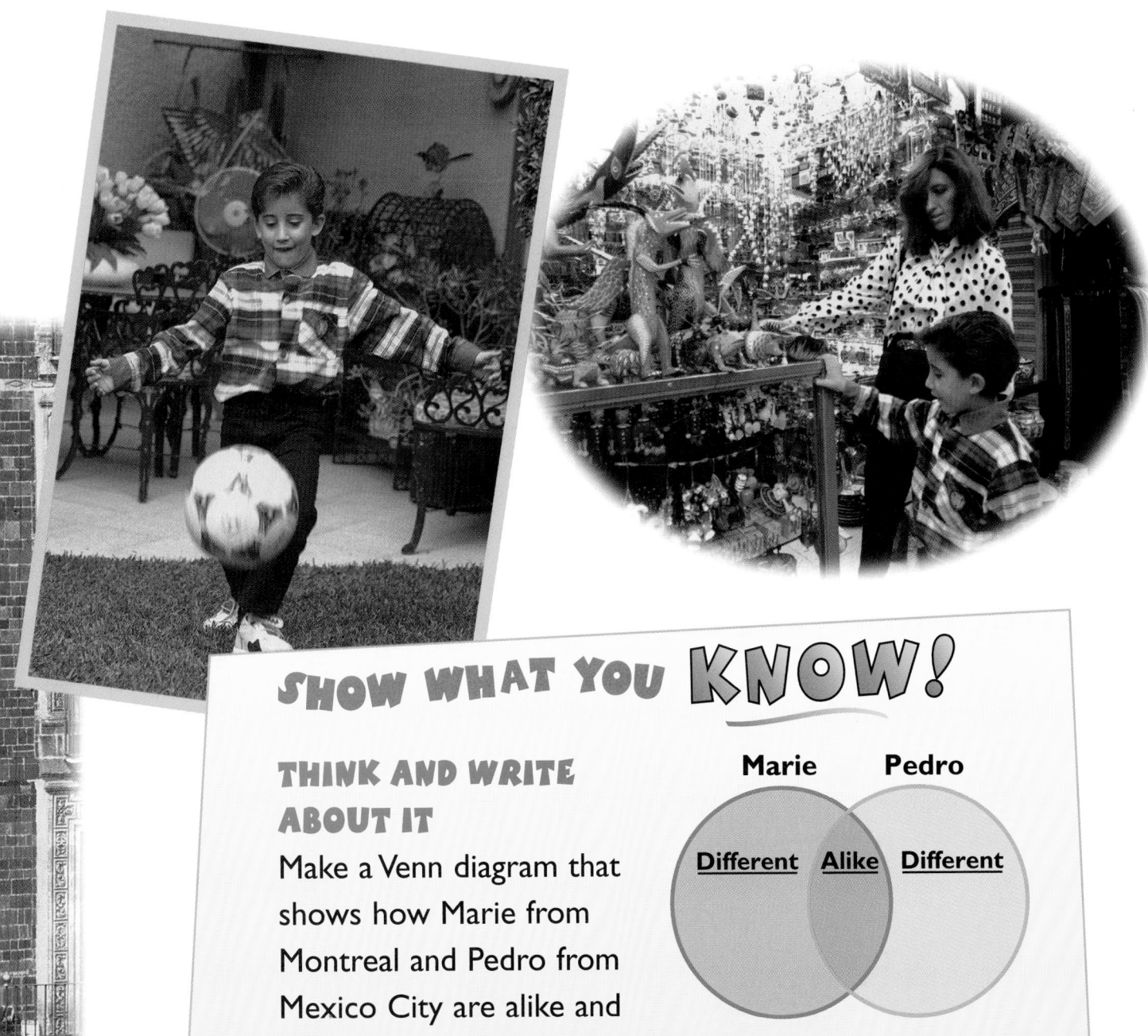

SHOW WHAT YOU KNOW!

THINK AND WRITE ABOUT IT

Make a Venn diagram that shows how Marie from Montreal and Pedro from Mexico City are alike and different.

Marie   Pedro

Different   Alike   Different

Communication Then and Now

Communication Today

Meet Christina from Los Angeles, California, and Jeremy from Sydney, Australia. How do these friends, who live thousands of miles apart, **communicate**, or give each other messages? They don't use the telephone—they use home computers.

The written messages these friends send travel between their computers within a few seconds. To Christina and Jeremy, computers make it seem as if they were next-door neighbors.

Jeremy Moore
10 Harbor Avenue
Sydney, Australia NSW 2000

Christina Moreno
130 Seventh Street
Los Angeles, CA 90000

April 4

Dear Christina,
Did you know that more people live in Sydney than in any other city in Australia? My city has one of the biggest bridges in the world, too. Last weekend my family and I went to a fair. We saw the circus and listened to music. I had fun. My mom and dad told me that this fair has been held in Sydney each spring for more than 100 years.
How are you? Write me back soon.
Your friend,
Jeremy

Getting to Know Each Another

Christina and Jeremy also send handwritten messages to each other. Jeremy likes to write letters telling Christina what his city is like. Christina sends postcards to Jeremy with pictures of places she visits on vacation.

Sometimes Christina and Jeremy use a facsimile, or fax, machine to send drawings. Since they have not met in person, they learn about each other through their drawings, postcards, and letters.

Dear Jeremy,
My family and I are spending our vacation at Yellowstone National Park. We are having fun hiking and camping. The mountains are so big!
When I get home, I will draw you a picture of our vacation and fax it to you.
Your friend,
Christina

To: Jeremy Moore
10 Harbor Avenue
Sydney, Australia
NSW 2000

Communicating From Los Angeles to Sydney

ASIA
NORTH AMERICA
UNITED STATES
Los Angeles
PACIFIC OCEAN
SOUTH AMERICA
AUSTRALIA
Sydney
ANTARCTICA

① Fax picture to Jeremy
② Mail Jeremy's birthday card

▲ Cave painting

▲ Wedge-shaped symbols

▼ Egyptian pictures and symbols

Communication Long Ago

Thousands of years ago, people shared ideas by painting pictures on cave walls. Later, people drew pictures and symbols that stood for objects and sounds.

Some people drew symbols on wet clay tablets. Then the tablets were dried in the sun. The people of Egypt, called Egyptians, wrote pictures, symbols, and stories on building walls.

▲ Chinese writing looks like pictures.

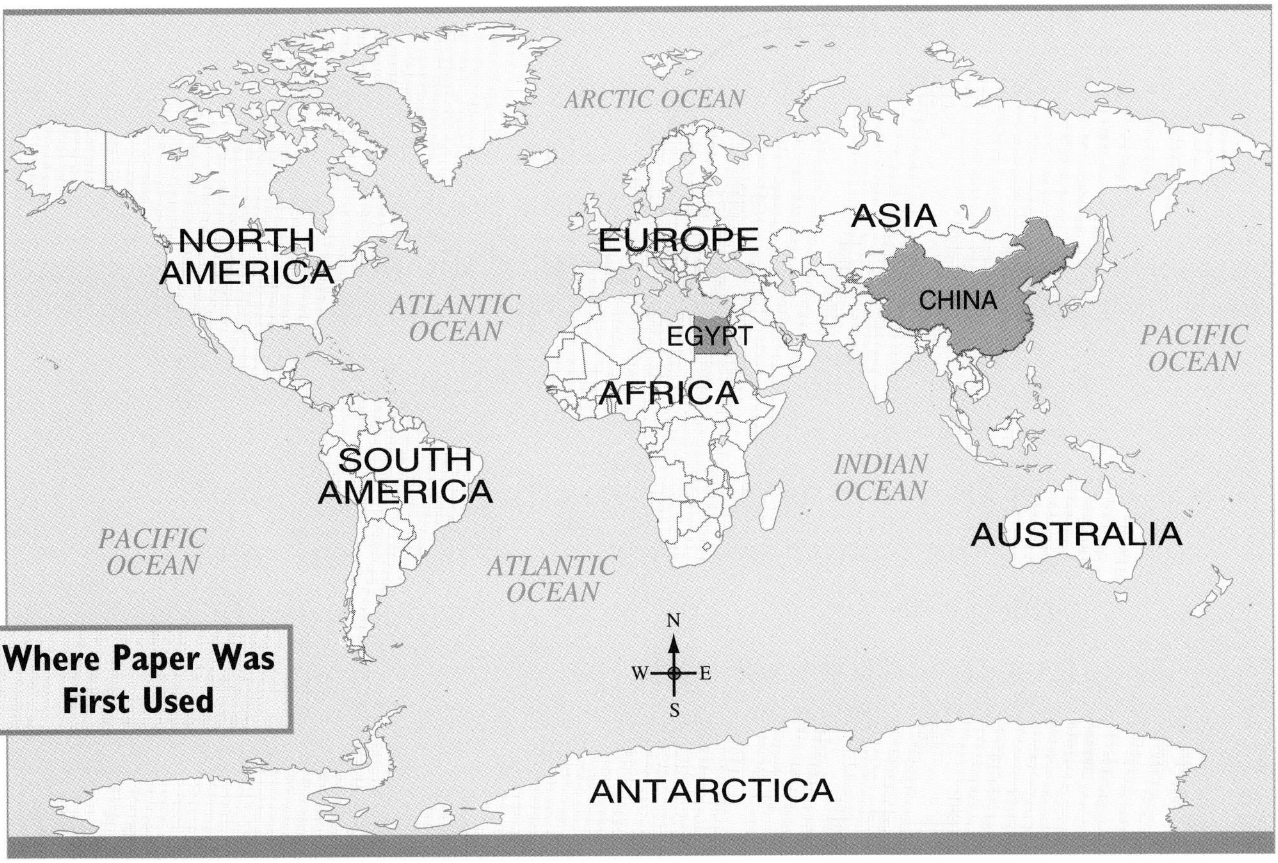

Where Paper Was First Used

NORTH AMERICA

SOUTH AMERICA

EUROPE

ASIA

CHINA

EGYPT

AFRICA

AUSTRALIA

ANTARCTICA

ARCTIC OCEAN

ATLANTIC OCEAN

PACIFIC OCEAN

PACIFIC OCEAN

ATLANTIC OCEAN

INDIAN OCEAN

N
W E
S

Picture Writing From Egypt and China

	Egypt	China
Sun		
Mountain		
Man		
Rain		
Fish		
Stars		

The Invention of Paper

People also wrote on stone, wood, and animal skins. The Egyptians wrote on a thin paperlike material made from tall grass.

Later the Chinese invented paper. Paper made it easier for people who lived far away to communicate. This was because paper was lighter to carry than stone or wood. The map on this page shows where paper was first used.

113

The Printing Press and Other Inventions

More than 1,500 years ago, people began to make books on the continent of Europe. But this took a lot of time because every book was written by hand. Finally a machine called the printing press was invented. Today we still use printing presses to make books, magazines, and newspapers.

In 1876 the typewriter was invented. Then came the computer. At first, a computer was so big it filled one whole room. Now, a computer can fit right on your school desk.

The printing press was invented more than 500 years ago. ▼

A model of the first typewriter ▲

More Inventions

More inventions for communication are being made. You may have used a CD-ROM. This is a computer program that has words, pictures, and music. People have gone from cave art to computers. How do you think you will communicate with your friends in the future?

SHOW WHAT YOU KNOW!

WRITE ABOUT IT AND DRAW IT

Write a short message by drawing pictures and symbols that stand for important words. Then share your message with a classmate.

Key Word
folk dance

Around the

Dancing to Tell Stories

"Aloha" and hello. My name is Luka. I dance the dance of my mother, my grandmother, and her mother before her. When I dance the hula, I tell a story just by moving my hips and hands. My grass skirt makes a sound like wind in a palm tree. And my hands move like a flying bird.

In Hawaii, it is important that the young children learn the dances of our ancestors. These dances are a part of our Hawaiian history. The map below will help you find Hawaii and the other places that you will read about in this lesson.

▲ Dancing the hula

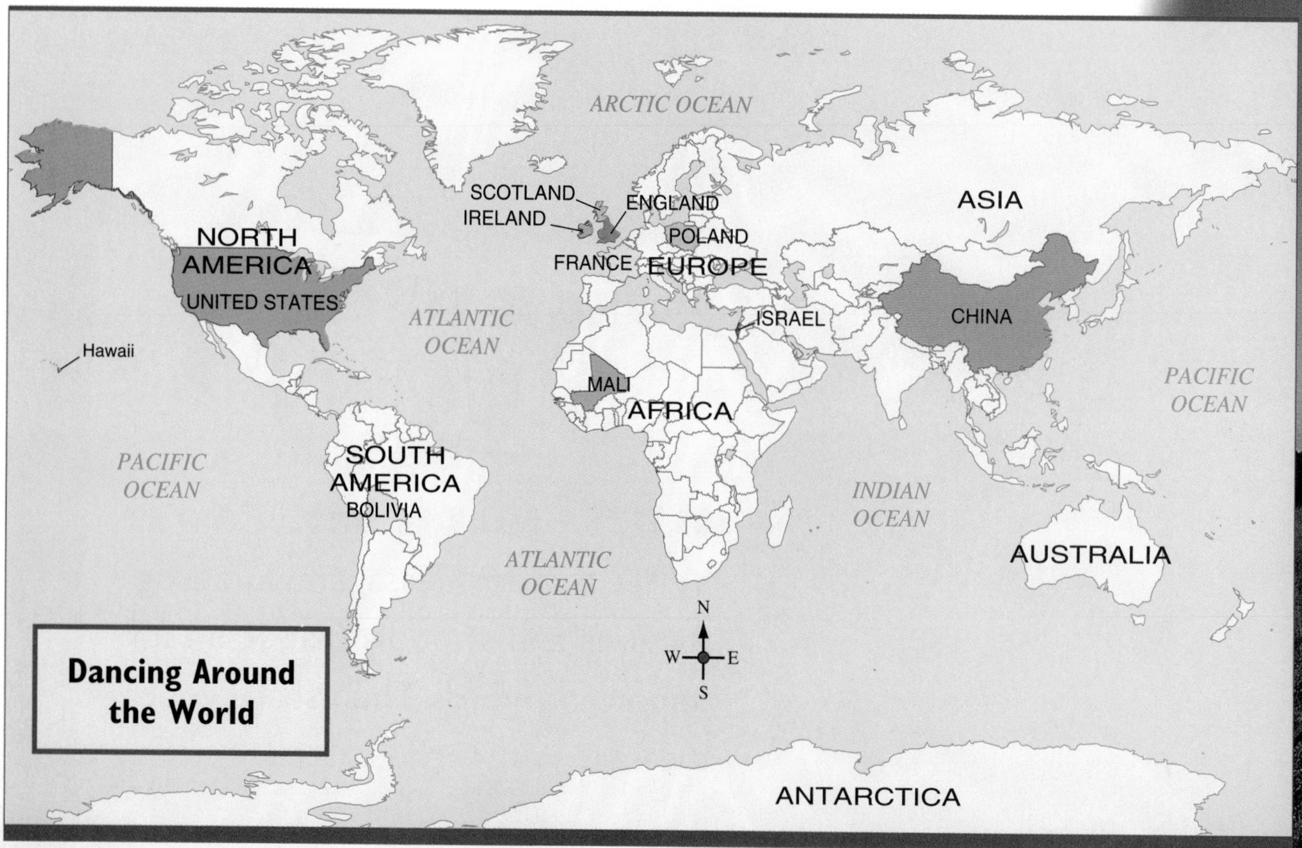

Dancing Around the World

(World map showing: ARCTIC OCEAN; NORTH AMERICA, UNITED STATES, Hawaii; SOUTH AMERICA, BOLIVIA; SCOTLAND, IRELAND, ENGLAND, POLAND, FRANCE, EUROPE, ISRAEL; ASIA, CHINA; MALI, AFRICA; AUSTRALIA; ANTARCTICA; ATLANTIC OCEAN, PACIFIC OCEAN, INDIAN OCEAN; compass rose N, S, E, W)

World in Dance

Dancing to Celebrate

For thousands of years, people have danced to celebrate good harvests and hunting seasons. Long ago, African and Native American people dressed up and danced like the animals they hunted. They did this to bring good luck.

Today, people dance these dances as a celebration to remember the past. Dancers wear animal masks. They sing, chant, and tell the stories of the hunters of long ago. And they shake rattles and beat drums as they twist and turn.

A dancer from Mali wears an animal mask. ▶

▲ In France, men called shepherds perform a dance on stilts as they celebrate.

Dancing for Other Reasons

Around the world, people dance for many other reasons. Some dance to make their work more pleasant. Others dance to welcome springtime, to ask for rain to keep crops growing, or to celebrate the New Year. Some dances celebrate a birthday, a wedding, or a special holiday. Dancing together helps people feel that they are part of a community.

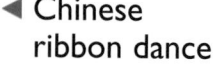
◀ Chinese ribbon dance

Dancers celebrating a holiday in Bolivia ▼

118

Dancing in the United States

When people come to live in the United States, they bring the dances of their countries with them. Have you ever danced the polka, a dance from Poland? Have you danced the hora, from Israel? Did you know that square dancing comes from English, Irish, and Scottish folk dances? A **folk dance** is passed down to people from their ancestors.

Dances often change along the way. But whether people dance the same steps or make up new ones, dance is a part of who we are.

Square dancing in
▼ the United States

SHOW WHAT YOU KNOW!

THINK ABOUT IT AND DANCE

Think of a special day that you celebrate in school. Make up a dance for it. Play music, sing or chant, beat a drum, and celebrate!

119

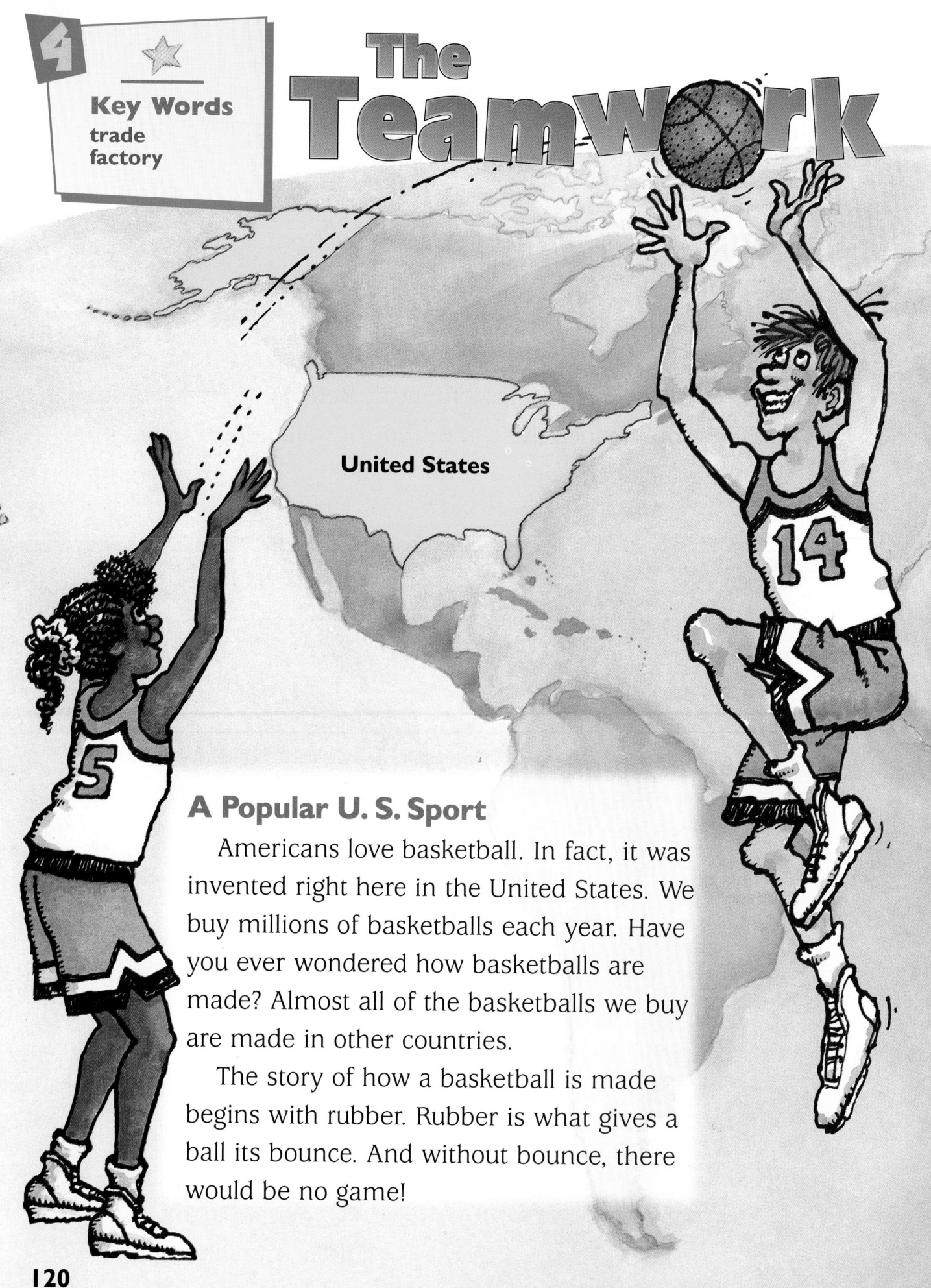

Key Words
trade
factory

The Teamwork

United States

A Popular U. S. Sport

Americans love basketball. In fact, it was invented right here in the United States. We buy millions of basketballs each year. Have you ever wondered how basketballs are made? Almost all of the basketballs we buy are made in other countries.

The story of how a basketball is made begins with rubber. Rubber is what gives a ball its bounce. And without bounce, there would be no game!

120

# of Trade

1 Rubber trees have a white juice that is used to make rubber. ▶

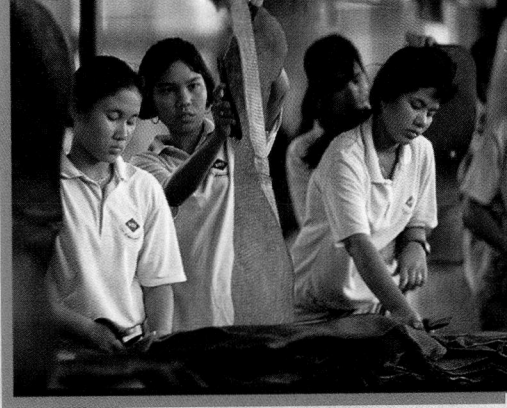

2 Workers checking sheets of rubber ▶

China

Thailand

What Is Trade?

Trade is the buying and selling of goods. Let's follow the bouncing basketball to see how basketballs are made and traded.

Rubber trees grow best in a hot and rainy place, such as Thailand. People drain a milky white juice from these trees. This juice is taken to a building where it is turned into sheets of rubber. From there the rubber is shipped to China.

121

3

◄ Sheets of rubber
ready to be shipped

4

A core being covered
with thread ►

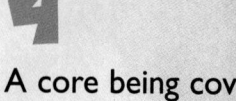

5

▲ The cores being
painted with glue

From Thailand to China

Once the rubber has been
shipped from Thailand to China,
it is cut into pieces in a factory,
or a building where products are
made. The pieces are glued
together to make thin, round
cores that go inside basketballs.

The cores are checked for air
leaks. Next, they are covered with
thread and more rubber to make
them stronger. Then, they are
painted with glue.

From China to the United States

The basketballs are almost finished. But leather must still be put on the outsides of the cores. Leather is cut into pieces. Then the pieces are glued onto the outsides. Finally, the finished basketballs are put into boxes and shipped from China to the United States.

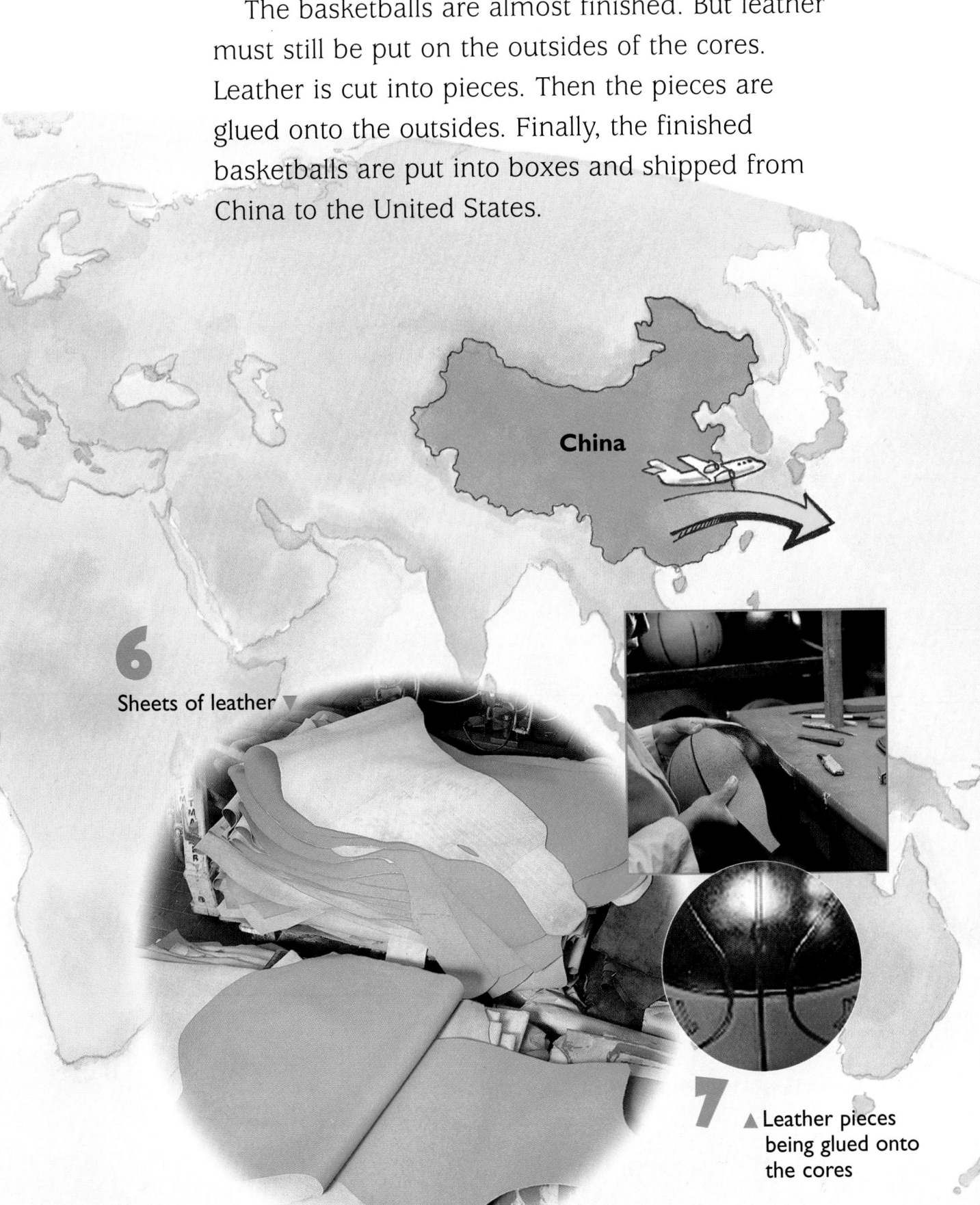

China

6
Sheets of leather ▼

7 ▲ Leather pieces being glued onto the cores

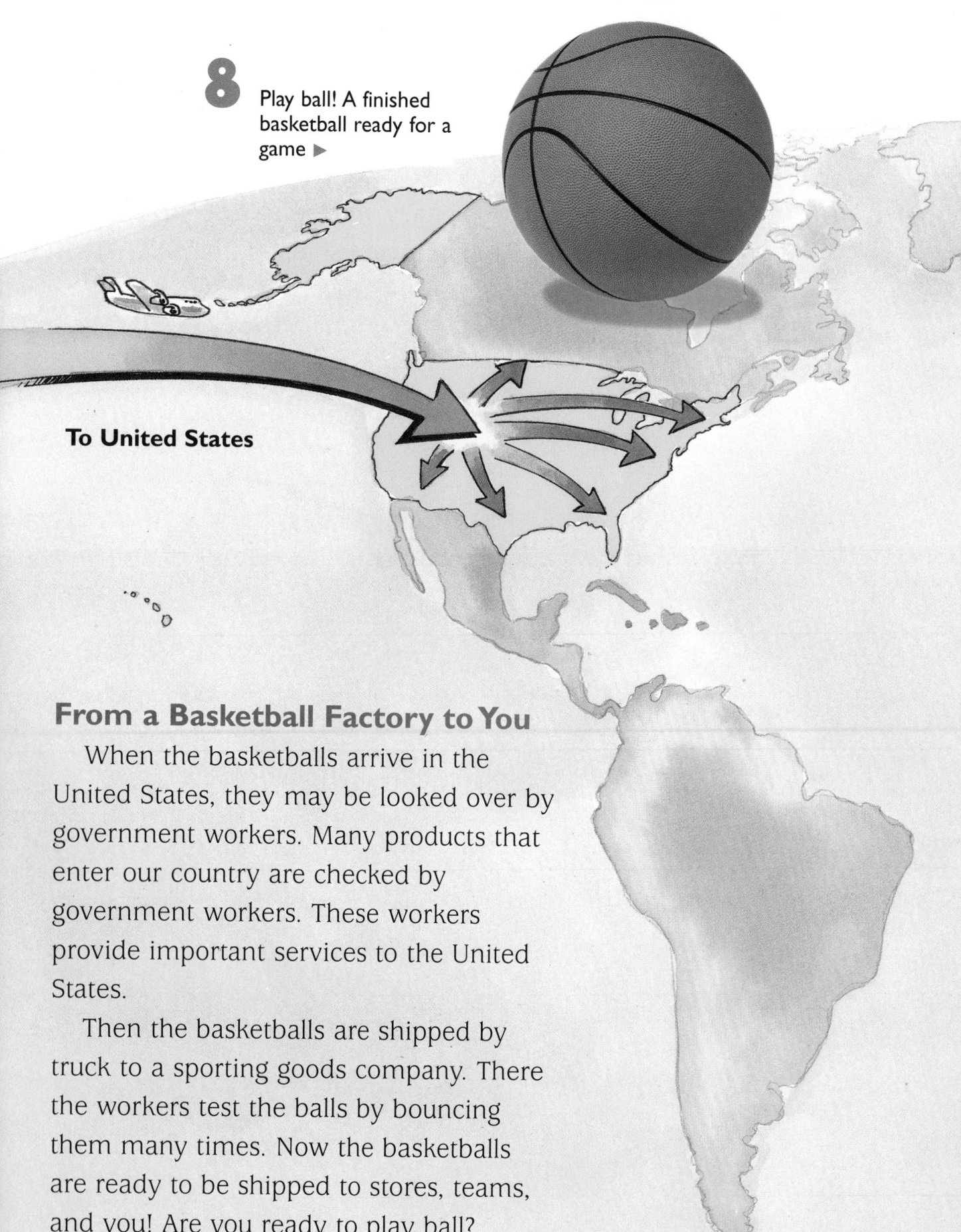

8 Play ball! A finished basketball ready for a game ▶

To United States

From a Basketball Factory to You

When the basketballs arrive in the United States, they may be looked over by government workers. Many products that enter our country are checked by government workers. These workers provide important services to the United States.

Then the basketballs are shipped by truck to a sporting goods company. There the workers test the balls by bouncing them many times. Now the basketballs are ready to be shipped to stores, teams, and you! Are you ready to play ball?

Teamwork Is What It Takes

The next time you bounce a basketball, think about where it came from. Remember, it takes the teamwork of countries to make basketballs. And it takes the teamwork of basketball players to make the game happen.

SHOW WHAT YOU KNOW!

THINK ABOUT IT AND MAKE A CHART

Work with a classmate. Look at the pictures in this lesson and draw a flowchart showing how a basketball is made.

Landmarks Around The World

A Landmark of Liberty

Grab your camera! It's time to visit some of the world's most famous landmarks. A landmark is a structure that helps you find or recognize a place.

Let's begin with the Statue of Liberty. This huge statue stands on an island in New York Harbor. In 1884, France gave the statue to the United States as a sign of its friendship. Since then many people have come to the United States to live. For them the statue stands for hope and freedom. Today many people visit this landmark because freedom is important to them.

Fun Fact

The Statue of Liberty was built in France and then taken apart and shipped to the United States in about 300 pieces.

Landmarks Old and New

Landmarks can be old, such as Machu Picchu, in Peru. This amazing city was home to a group of people called the Incas. It was forgotten for hundreds of years until the remains of the city were uncovered about 85 years ago.

Unlike Machu Picchu, the Sydney Opera House, in Australia, is new. This building looks like a ship with many sails. People from around the world go there to hear music and watch dancing.

Fun Facts

Machu Picchu was hidden under trees for many years.

The Sydney Opera House took 15 years to build.

A Landmark Built for Safety

If you were in an airplane looking down at China, you might think that you were looking at a giant snake! The Great Wall of China, the world's longest wall, winds around 4,000 miles. It was built more than 2,000 years ago to keep the citizens of China safe from people wanting to take over the country.

Fun Fact

About 1 million people built the Great Wall of China.

Some Amazing Landmarks

Some landmarks look as if they would last forever, but the Parthenon isn't one of them. The Parthenon stands on a hilltop in Greece. It was built more than 2,000 years ago. Although only ruins of the building remain today, the Parthenon is so admired that many buildings in the United States have been made to look like it.

The Egyptian pyramids are much older and stronger. These huge four-sided stone structures were tombs for the kings of Egypt. It took thousands of people to build one pyramid. Today, people wonder how the Egyptians were able to build the pyramids without machines and modern tools.

Fun Fact

It is against the law to take even a pebble from the Parthenon.

Fun Fact

The average weight of each of the stone blocks used to build the Egyptian pyramids is more than two tons.

129

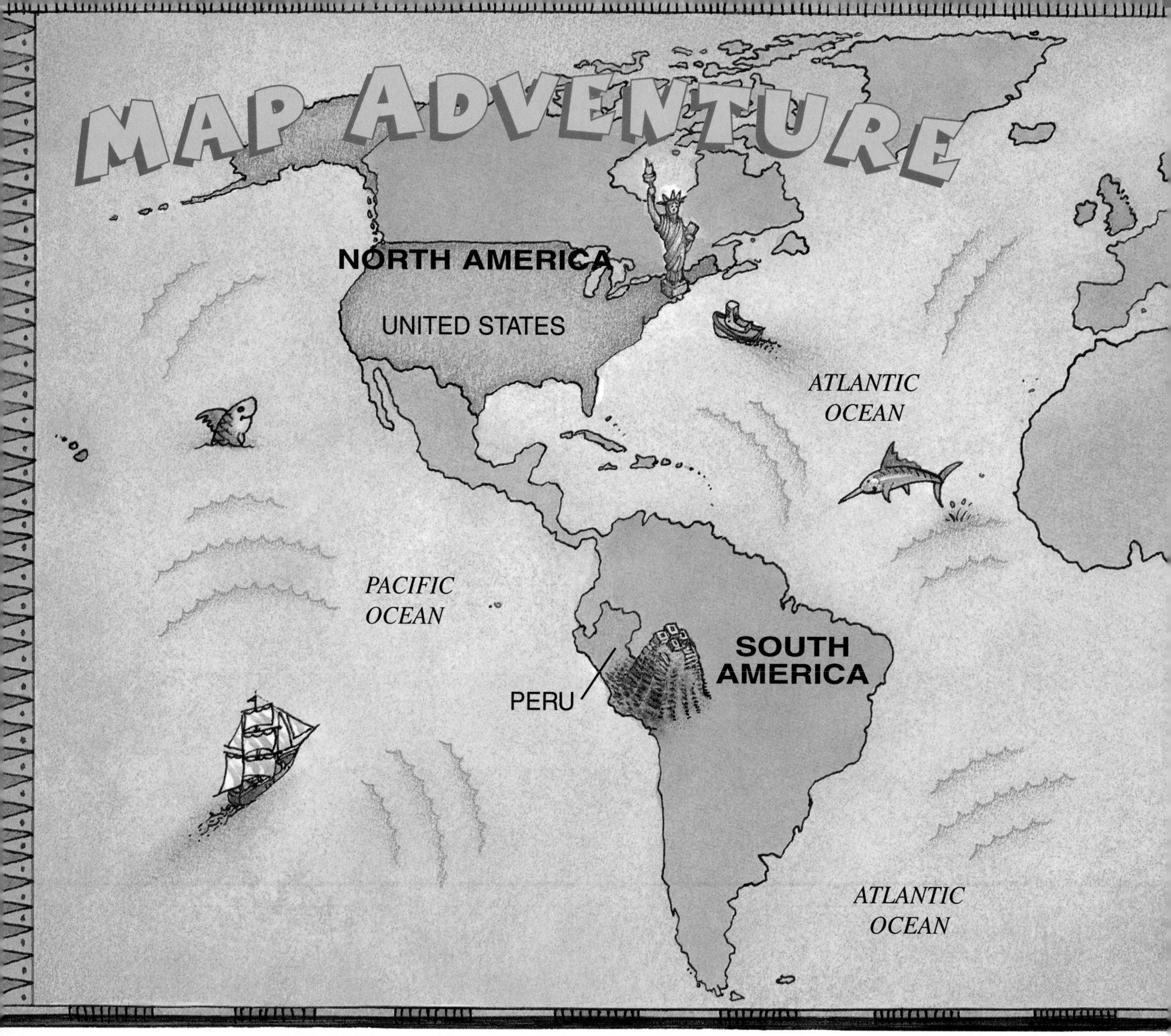

MAP ADVENTURE

NORTH AMERICA

UNITED STATES

ATLANTIC OCEAN

PACIFIC OCEAN

PERU

SOUTH AMERICA

ATLANTIC OCEAN

World Landmarks

The map shows you where each of the landmarks you've just read about is found.

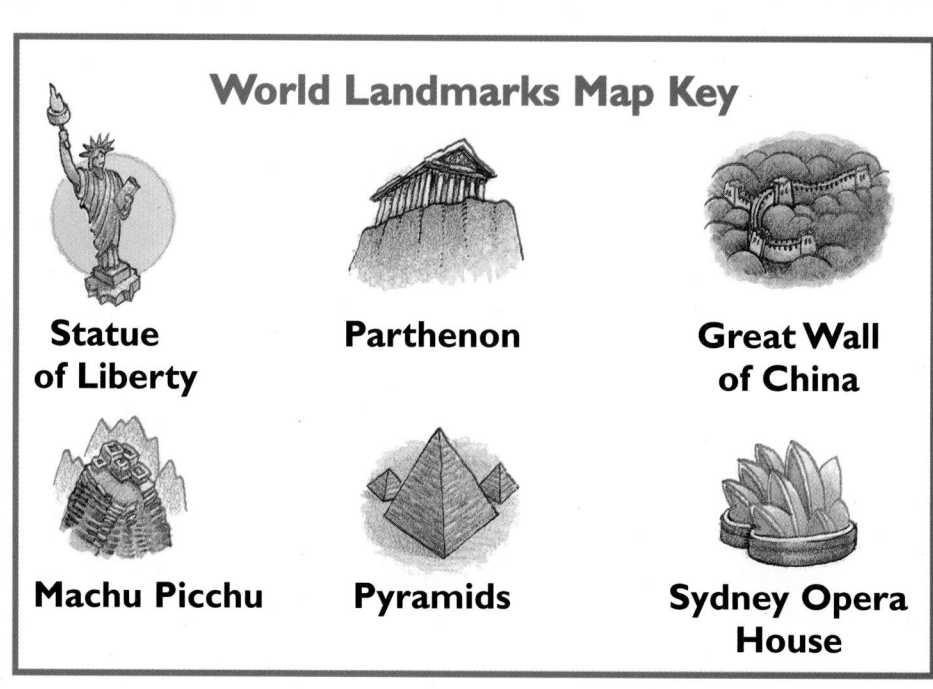

World Landmarks Map Key

Statue of Liberty

Parthenon

Great Wall of China

Machu Picchu

Pyramids

Sydney Opera House

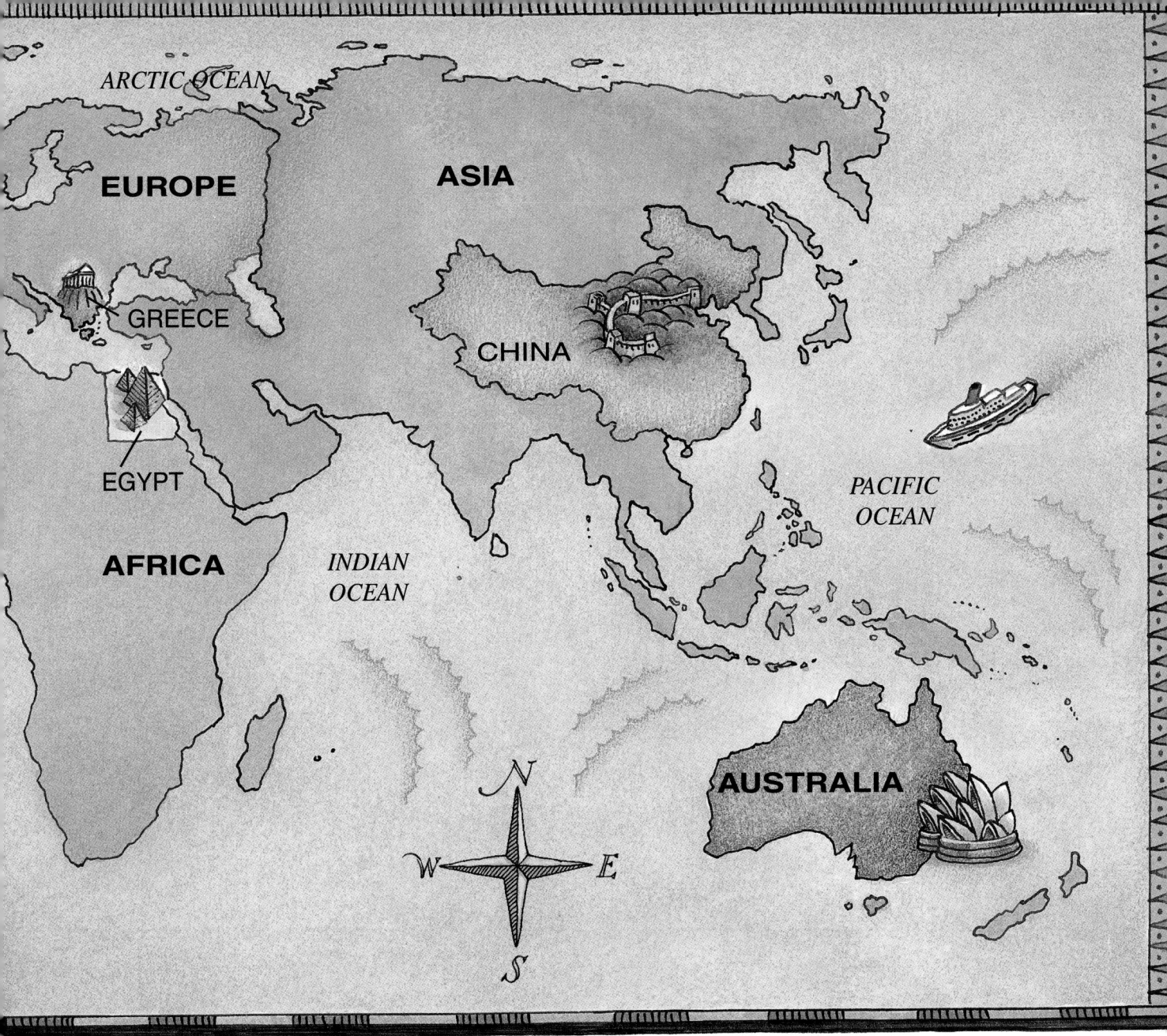

SHOW WHAT YOU KNOW!

MAP IT

Study the map and the map key. Then write the names of the country and continent on which each landmark is located.

EXPLORE IT

Plan a trip around the world to visit all the landmarks. Decide the shortest way to go. Then trace the route you've chosen. Enjoy your trip!

Key Word
storytellers

Stories Tell Our History

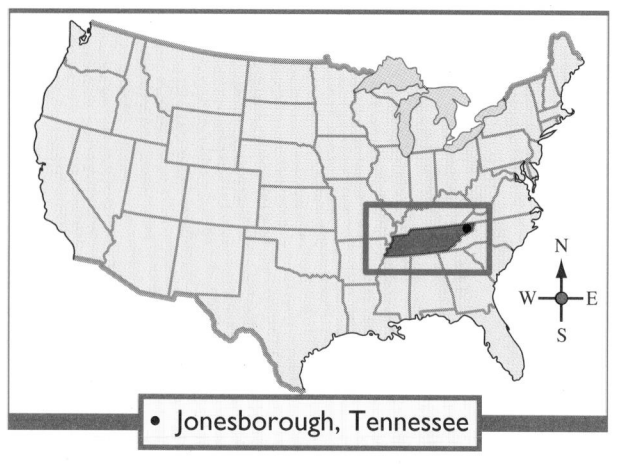

• Jonesborough, Tennessee

Once Upon a Time

Our last stop is Jonesborough, Tennessee. Every October, thousands of people visit the National Storytelling Festival. Under big tents, **storytellers** from across the United States share their tales. Some share stories about their families and ancestors who lived in different places around the world. These stories tell the histories of people and places near and far. Some of the stories begin, as good stories often do, with "Once upon a time."

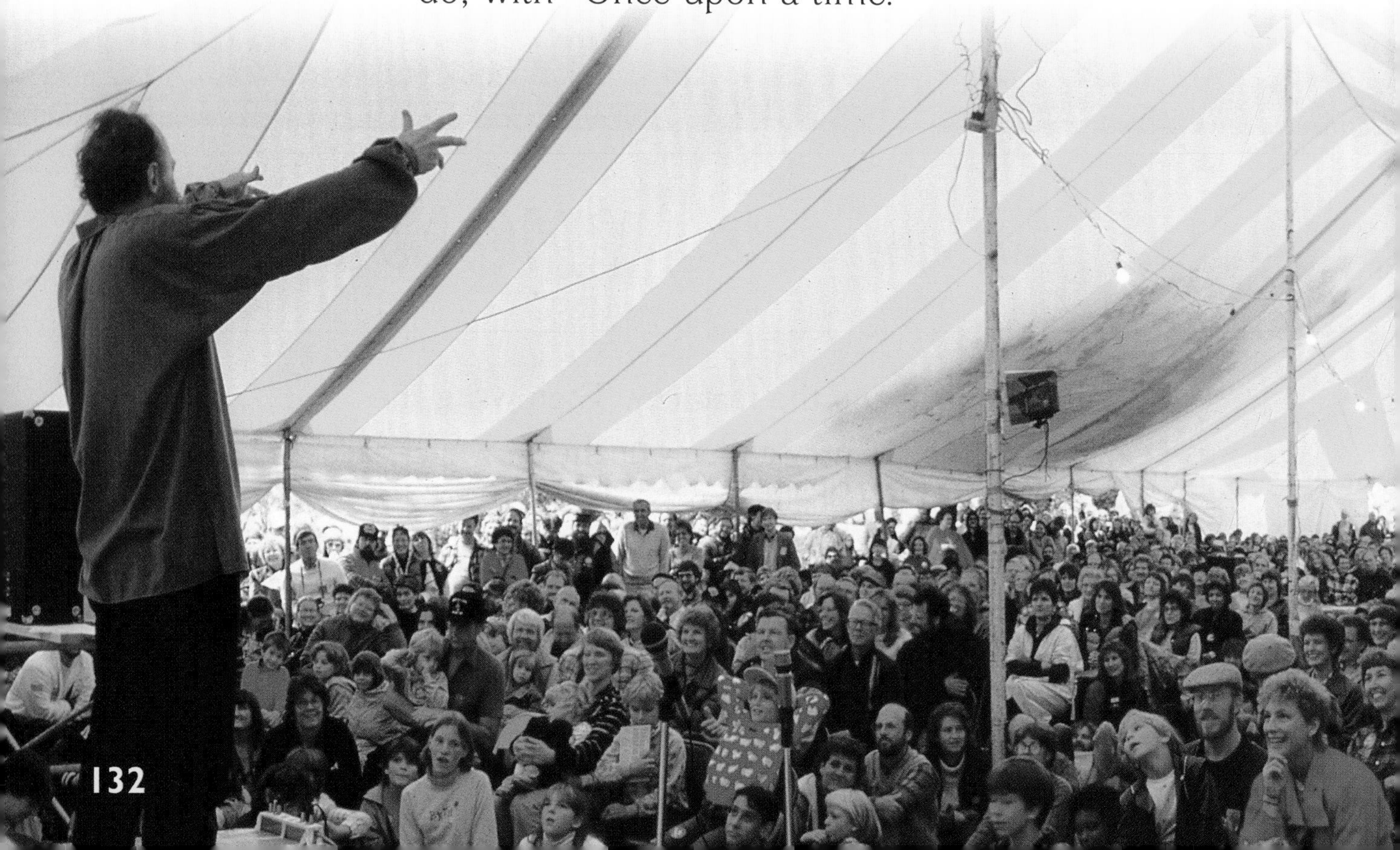

All Kinds of Stories

People have always told stories. They drew them on cave walls, on clay tablets, and on animal skins. They told tales by firelight and on front porches. Some made-up stories are called fairy tales. Some stories, called fables, have lessons to share. Still other stories tell about real people and places. For thousands of years, people have spoken, sung, and danced stories about themselves and their ancestors. Can you name a fairy tale or a fable?

▲ A storyteller may wear a costume and play instruments.

◄ This storyteller holds a fan as she tells her story.

A storyteller uses hoops to tell his story. ▶

Ways of Telling Stories

A storyteller beats a drum and invites his audience to chant along with him. Some storytellers play guitars or harmonicas. Some wear hats or paint their faces. And some tell their stories by using hoops or pieces of string.

Storytellers may invite us to clap, sing, and sign words to add to the fun of the stories. Some storytellers even invite children to help tell their stories.

▼ Playing music can help tell a story.

134

Listening to and Telling Stories

People come to Jonesborough from all over the United States to hear stories. People love listening to stories because they tell about who we are and where we come from. Telling stories can be a way of sharing your life with others. Now it's your turn. Begin your story, as many good stories do, with "Once upon a time."

SHOW WHAT YOU KNOW!

THINK AND TELL ABOUT IT

Think of a story you would like to tell. Decide what you need to help tell it. Practice telling your story to a classmate. Then share your story with your class.

SUMMING UP

1 DO YOU REMEMBER . . .

1. Name one way Marie and Pedro are alike and one way they are different.

2. What are four ways that people have communicated with one another?

3. Name three reasons that people dance.

4. What is trade?

5. Tell about one of the landmarks you read about.

6. What are some props or things that storytellers use to tell their stories?

3 WHAT DO YOU THINK?

1. Describe how your life is like Marie's and Pedro's and how it is different, too.

2. Why was the invention of the printing press so important?

3. Why do we depend on another country for the rubber in basketballs?

4. Which landmark that you read about would you like to visit? Why?

2 USING YOUR SKILLS

Use the chart below to organize information about the locations of the landmarks in this theme.

Copy the chart and fill in the missing information.

Where's That Landmark?

Landmark	Country	Continent
1. Statue of Liberty	United States	North America
2. Machu Picchu		
3. Sydney Opera House	Australia	Australia
4. Great Wall of China		
5. Parthenon		
6. Pyramids		

ALL AROUND THE WORLD

4 USING YOUR WORDS

Write seven sentences. For each sentence, use one of the words listed below.

capital
communicate
factory
folk dance
landmark
storytellers
trade

5 YOU CAN READ MAPS

This map shows some of the cities and countries you read about. Choose five places that you would like to visit. Decide on a route and write directions to get from place to place.

ARCTIC OCEAN

CANADA
NORTH AMERICA • Montreal
UNITED STATES • Jonesborough
Los Angeles •
MEXICO
Mexico City ☆
Hawaii

EUROPE   ASIA
GREECE   CHINA
EGYPT   PACIFIC OCEAN
AFRICA   THAILAND

ATLANTIC OCEAN

PACIFIC OCEAN
PERU
SOUTH AMERICA

ATLANTIC OCEAN
INDIAN OCEAN
AUSTRALIA
• Sydney

Around the World
• Cities
⊛ National capital

N
W—◆—E
S

ANTARCTICA

137

THE WORLD

RUSSIA

Alaska
(UNITED STATES)

CANADA

Gree
(DEN

UNITED STATES OF AMERICA

ATLANTIC

OCEAN

MEXICO

CUBA

Puerto Rico
(UNITED STATES)

Hawaiian Is.
(UNITED STATES)

GUATEMALA
El Salvador

HONDURAS
NICARAGUA

PACIFIC

OCEAN

COSTA RICA
PANAMA

VENEZUELA

COLOMBIA

GUYANA
SURINAME
FRENCH GUIANA
(FRANCE)

ECUADOR

PERU

BRAZIL

BOLIVIA

PARAGUAY

CHILE

URUGUAY

NEW
ZEALAND

ARGENTINA

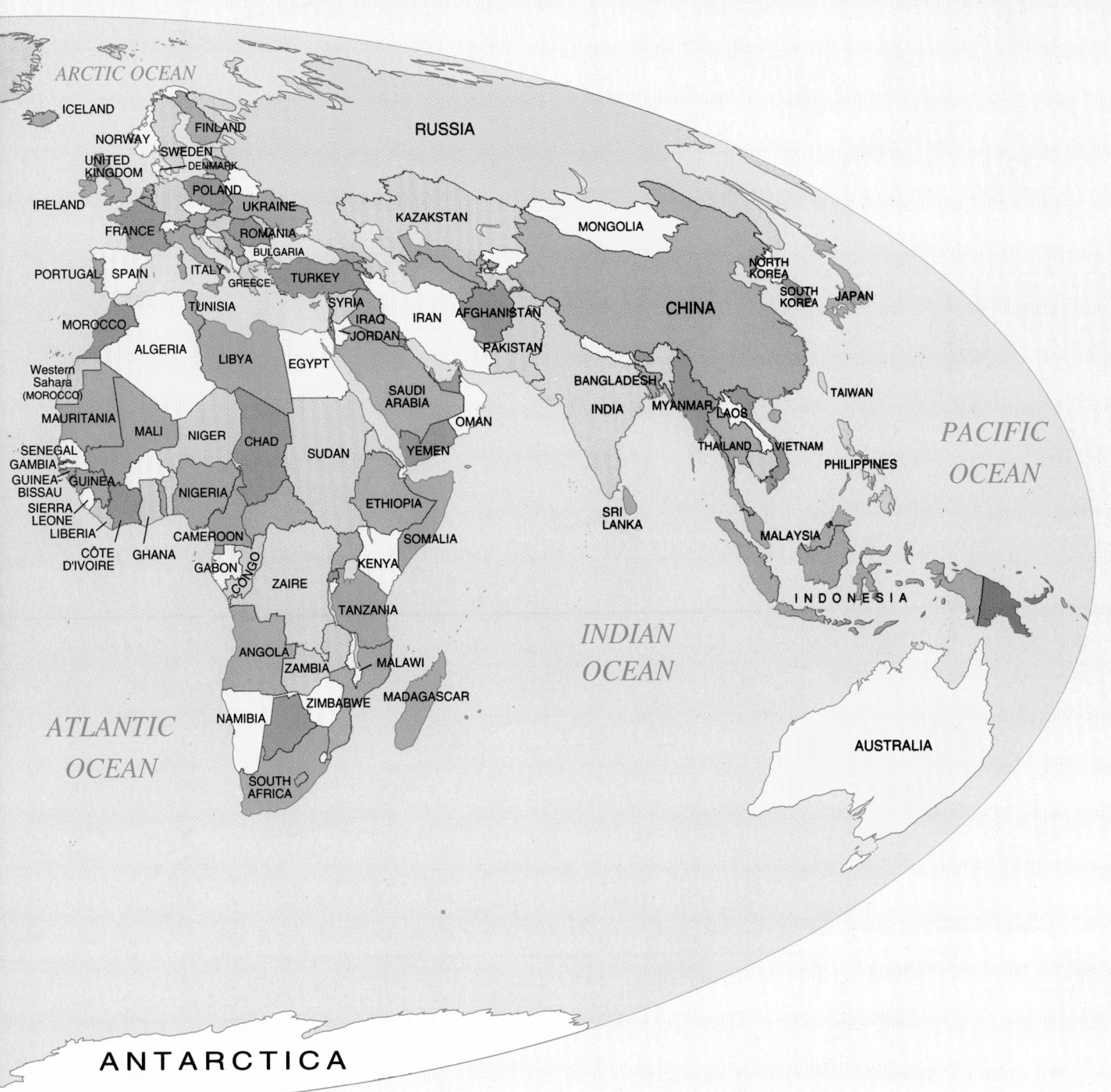

ARCTIC OCEAN

ICELAND

FINLAND

NORWAY

SWEDEN

DENMARK

UNITED KINGDOM

IRELAND

POLAND

RUSSIA

FRANCE

UKRAINE

KAZAKSTAN

MONGOLIA

ROMANIA

BULGARIA

PORTUGAL

SPAIN

ITALY

GREECE

TURKEY

NORTH KOREA

SOUTH KOREA

JAPAN

MOROCCO

TUNISIA

SYRIA

IRAQ

IRAN

AFGHANISTAN

CHINA

JORDAN

PAKISTAN

TAIWAN

ALGERIA

LIBYA

EGYPT

Western Sahara (MOROCCO)

SAUDI ARABIA

BANGLADESH

MAURITANIA

OMAN

INDIA

MYANMAR

LAOS

MALI

NIGER

CHAD

SUDAN

YEMEN

THAILAND

VIETNAM

SENEGAL

GAMBIA

GUINEA-BISSAU

GUINEA

NIGERIA

ETHIOPIA

PHILIPPINES

SIERRA LEONE

SRI LANKA

LIBERIA

CÔTE D'IVOIRE

GHANA

CAMEROON

SOMALIA

MALAYSIA

GABON

CONGO

ZAIRE

KENYA

INDONESIA

TANZANIA

PACIFIC OCEAN

ANGOLA

ZAMBIA

MALAWI

INDIAN OCEAN

ATLANTIC OCEAN

NAMIBIA

ZIMBABWE

MADAGASCAR

AUSTRALIA

SOUTH AFRICA

ANTARCTICA

RUSSIA

ALASKA

CANADA

Yukon River

Anchorage

PACIFIC OCEAN

Juneau

Seattle

Olympia ★ WASHINGTON

Columbia R.

Portland

Salem

OREGON

Helena ★

MONTANA

Missouri River

Billings

IDAHO

Boise ★

Snake River

Pocatello

WYOMING

Casper

PACIFIC OCEAN

Sacramento ★

Carson City ★

NEVADA

Great Salt Lake

Salt Lake City ★

Cheyenne ★

Denver ★

CALIFORNIA

UTAH

COLORADO

Colorado Springs

Las Vegas

Colorado River

Los Angeles

ARIZONA

Santa Fe ★

Albuquerque

NEW MEXICO

Phoenix ★

Honolulu ★

HAWAII

Tucson

MEXICO

United States

⊛ National capital

★ State capitals

• Other cities

CANADA

NORTH DAKOTA
★ Bismarck
• Fargo

MINNESOTA
Minneapolis • ★ St. Paul

SOUTH DAKOTA
★ Pierre
• Sioux Falls

WISCONSIN
Madison ★
• Milwaukee

MICHIGAN

Lake Superior

Lake Huron

Lake Michigan

MICHIGAN
★ Lansing
• Detroit

Lake Erie

Lake Ontario

IOWA
Cedar Rapids •
★ Des Moines

NEBRASKA
• Omaha
★ Lincoln

ILLINOIS
Chicago •
★ Springfield

Fort Wayne •

INDIANA
★ Indianapolis

OHIO
★ Columbus
Cleveland •

NEW YORK
Albany ★

VERMONT
Montpelier ★
Burlington •

MAINE
★ Augusta
• Portland

Concord ★ **NEW HAMPSHIRE**

Nashua •
Boston ★ **MASSACHUSETTS**
Plymouth •
Hartford ★ Providence ★
Warwick •
Bridgeport • **RHODE ISLAND**
CONNECTICUT

PENNSYLVANIA
Newark •
New York •
Harrisburg ★
Philadelphia •
Trenton ★ **NEW JERSEY**
Wilmington •
Baltimore • Dover ★ **DELAWARE**
Washington ⊛ Annapolis ★ **MARYLAND**
D.C.

WEST VIRGINIA
★ Charleston

VIRGINIA
Richmond ★

KANSAS
★ Topeka
• Wichita

MISSOURI
• Kansas City
★ Jefferson City
St. Louis •

Louisville •
★ Frankfort

KENTUCKY

OKLAHOMA
• Tulsa
★ Oklahoma City

ARKANSAS
Little Rock ★

Memphis •

Nashville •
TENNESSEE

NORTH CAROLINA
★ Raleigh
• Charlotte

SOUTH CAROLINA
Columbia ★
• Charleston

Ohio River

Mississippi River

Red River

TEXAS
★ Austin
• Houston

LOUISIANA
Baton Rouge ★
New Orleans •

Biloxi •

MISSISSIPPI
★ Jackson

Birmingham •
ALABAMA
Montgomery ★

Atlanta ★
GEORGIA
Columbus •

Tallahassee ★ • St. Augustine

FLORIDA

Brazos River

Rio Grande

Gulf of Mexico

ATLANTIC OCEAN

N
W ✦ E
S

Bering
Sea

ARCTIC OCEAN

Greenland
(Denmark)

ICELAND

Beaufort
Sea

Gulf of
Alaska

Great
Bear
Lake

Great
Slave Lake

Hudson
Bay

PACIFIC
OCEAN

CANADA

Winnipeg
Lake

Great
Salt
Lake

Great
Lakes

Ottawa ⊛

Toronto

Detroit

Boston

Chicago

New York

UNITED STATES

Philadelphia

San Francisco

Washington ⊛

OF AMERICA

ATLANTIC
OCEAN

Los Angeles

MEXICO

Gulf of Mexico

Miami

N

W ⊛ E

S

Guadalajara

Mexico
City ⊛

Caribbean
Sea

NORTH AMERICA

⊛ National capitals

• Other cities

SOUTH
AMERICA

PACIFIC
OCEAN

142

GLOSSARY

A

ancestor A family member who lived long ago. Tony's great-grandfather teaches him songs his **ancestors** sang long ago. p. 61.

apprentice A person learning a trade or craft from someone else. Jack can't wait until he becomes an **apprentice** so that he can learn how to make shoes in his father's shop. p. 47.

C

capital A city or town where leaders of a country make laws. The **capital** of Mexico is Mexico City. p. 108.

change When something does not stay the same. One **change** that I have noticed is how much taller I've gotten since last year. p. 40.

citizen A member of a country. Michael is a good **citizen** because he has helped many people in his community. p. 28.

city A large community. A **city** has many homes and buildings, museums, stores, and lots of fun things to do. p. 40.

colony A community that is ruled by a country far away. The king of England made up laws for people living in far-away **colonies**. p. 66.

communicate To give information. Christina and Jeremy **communicate** by sending messages on their computers. p. 110.

ancestor

change

city

community A place where people live, work, and play. Rachel's **community** includes a school, a park, and a museum. p. 4.

conflict A situation caused by different ideas and feelings. Kareem and I had a **conflict** because he never lets me pitch. p. 14.

consumer A person who buys food and other goods. We are **consumers** because we buy food, clothing, books, and toys. p. 87.

consumer

custom The special way a group of people does something. My family enjoys the **custom** of eating pizza together every Friday night. p. 20.

D

document A printed paper that has information. The Declaration of Independence is an important **document** because it said that the colonists wanted to be free. p. 66.

E

earth The planet that is the home to all living things. The **earth** is like a big home where people, animals, and plants live together. p. 76.

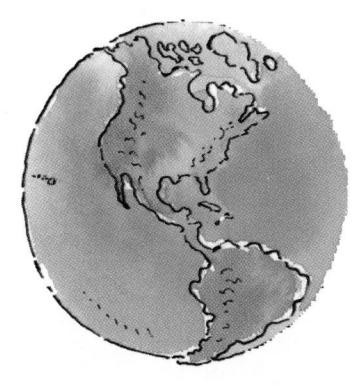

earth

endangered Plants and animals that are in danger of dying out. The giant pandas are **endangered** because they don't have enough food to eat. p. 88.

environment A place where a specific mix of plants and animals live. The dry desert and the wet rain forest are two **environments** found on the earth. p. 80.

extinct Having died out; no longer living. Dinosaurs are **extinct**, but their bones can be found in museums. p. 88.

extinct

factory A place where products are made. A basketball is made in a **factory**. p. 122.

folk dance A kind of dance that comes from a particular group of people. The hora is a **folk dance** that many people in Israel like to do. p. 119.

freedom Being able to choose how we live. The Pilgrims wanted their **freedom** so that they could choose their own religion. p. 63.

harvest To pick or gather food when it is ripe or ready. Corn is ready to be **harvested** by fall. p. 85.

harvest

history All events that have happened in the past. Jack shared the **history** of how people lived in Williamsburg long ago. p. 44.

independence Being free from another, such as another country. **Independence** was important to the people of Texas because they wanted to be free from Mexico. p. 51.

landmark A structure that is important to a particular place. The Statue of Liberty is an important **landmark** in the United States that is visited by people from around the world. p. 126.

landmark

145

law A rule that people must follow or obey. There are many **laws**, such as stop at stop signs, that people obey in Rachel's community. p. 6.

M

map key

map key A part of a map that explains the symbols used on a map. Use the **map key** to help you locate important places on the map. p. 9.

N

natural resource Something found in nature that people use. **Natural resources**, such as water and air, are needed so that people can live. p. 76.

neighborhood A part of a community. Teresa lives in Chinatown, a **neighborhood** that is a part of the city of San Francisco. p. 54.

P

personal history The story of a person's life. Kim's **personal history** includes pictures of her as a baby and as a soccer player today. p. 43.

polluted

polluted Unclean or dirty land, air, or water. Our rivers and oceans become **polluted** when people throw garbage into them. p. 96.

problem A difficult situation or issue that needs to be solved or answered. It was a **problem** when there wasn't a bicycle helmet law to help prevent injuries. p. 29.

protect To keep from danger. Police officers **protect** people. p. 13.

pueblo This word means "town" in Spanish. The Taos **pueblo** is the community in which Tony and his family live. p. 60.

R

rain forest A place that is warm and wet and has many plants and animals. The **rain forest** is home to many trees, plants, birds, and animals. p. 80.

recycle To process and reuse materials, such as glass. It is important to **recycle** paper so that fewer trees are cut down each year. p. 95.

reduce To lessen in amount. **Reduce** the amount of paper you use by writing on the back of each sheet. p. 95.

resolve To solve or settle a problem. We can **resolve** the problem by talking and listening to each other. p. 16.

reuse To extend the life of an object by using it again or in a new way. I can **reuse** a plastic cup by washing it and using it again. p. 95.

rule What people should and should not do. Rachel reminded Richie of important **rules** to follow in their home. p. 4.

S

senator A lawmaker. The **senator** helped to pass important laws that protect our environment. p. 97.

pueblo

recycle

senator

solution An answer to a problem. The children found a **solution** by helping to pass a bicycle safety law. p. 30.

storyteller A person who tells stories. Some **storytellers** wear costumes and play drums when they tell their stories. p. 132.

T ━━━━━━━━━━━━━━━━━━━━━━━━

trade To buy, sell, or exchange goods or services. I would like to **trade** my basketball for your soccer ball. p. 121.

trade

tradition Something that is done a certain way for many years. Important **traditions** in Tony's pueblo include dancing, singing, and baking bread. p. 60

W ━━━━━━━━━━━━━━━━━━━━━━━━

waterway A body of water, such as a river, a lake, or a stream. **Waterways** are bodies of water in which fish live. p. 78.

waterway

ACKNOWLEDGMENTS AND CREDITS

Special thanks are given to the following: The Colonial Williamsburg Foundation, Williamsburg, Virginia; the Dover Police Department, Dover, New Jersey; the Center for Marine Conservation, Atlantic Regional Office, Pollution Prevention Program; Kim Curry, Michael John Kelly, Teresa Mao, Tony Martinez, and their families; Elliott Smith and Marcia Keegan.

Front Cover *Design, Art Direction, and Production:* Design Five, NYC; *Photo by* Dana Sigall. *Details by* Bob Pool/Tom Stack & Associates; Partridge Films Ltd./Oxford Scientific Films/Animals Animals; Kunio Owaki/The Stock Market; S. Trummer/The Image Bank; © Jeff Greenberg/Photo Researchers, Inc.; Gordon R. Gainer/The Stock Market.

Maps Ortelius Design.

All photographs by Silver Burdett Ginn (SBG) unless otherwise noted.

Photographs *Opposite* 1: Superstock; *t.m.* Jeff Greenberg/PhotoEdit; *t.r.* Phil Borden/PhotoEdit; *b.r.* Superstock. 21: *t.* Myrleen Ferguson/PhotoEdit. 26: Dino Vournas. 28: Dino Vournas for SBG. 29: *b.* Elliott Smith for SBG. 34: Everett Johnson/Leo de Wys. 35: Jeff Greenberg/PhotoEdit. 36: *t.* Elliott Smith for SBG; *b.* Marcia Keegan for SBG. 41: Courtesy, Brenda Curry. 42: *t.l.* Courtesy, Brenda Curry. 45–49: Colonial Williamsburg Foundation/SBG. 50: *t.* Steve Vidler/Leo de Wys. 51: *l.* Jim Markham; *r.* The Bettmann Archive. 52: Ron Thomas/FPG International. 53: Bob Daemmrich/Stock Boston. 54–55: Elliott Smith for SBG. 56–57: Elliott Smith for SBG. 57: *bkgd.* Deborah Davis/PhotoEdit; *inset* Elliott Smith for SBG. 61: *t.* Marcia Keegan for SBG; *b.* Marcia Keegan for SBG. 62: Marcia Keegan for SBG. 64: The Granger Collection, New York. 65: *t.* Bob Daemmrich/Stock Boston; *b.* Superstock. 66: The Granger Collection, New York. 67: Elliott Smith. 68: *l.* Vernon Merritt/Black Star; *r.* David Young Wolff/PhotoEdit. 70: *b.l.* Marcia Keegan for SBG; *b.r.* Elliott Smith for SBG. 76–77: Rich Buzzelli/Tom Stack & Associates. 78: Tammy Peluso/Tom Stack & Associates. 79: *l.* Dorey Sparre for SBG; *r.* Thomas Kitchin/Tom Stack & Associates. 80: Stanley Breeden/DRK Photo. 81: *t.l.* Zig Leszczynski/Animals Animals; *t.r.* Partridge Films Ltd./Oxford Scientific Films/Animals Animals; *b.* David M. Dennis/Tom Stack & Associates. 84–85: David M. Dennis/Tom Stack &

Associates. 85: *r.* Jim Foster/The Stock Market. 86: *bkgd.* Greg Ryan & Sally Beyer/Positive Reflections. 87: *t.* Elliott Smith for SBG; *b.* Elliott Smith for SBG. 89: Luiz C. Marigo/Peter Arnold. 90: Kim Heacox/DRK Photo. 91: Lynn M. Stone/Animals Animals. 92: © Bill Bachman/Photo Researchers, Inc. 93: Ray Pfortner/Peter Arnold. 94: *l.* Joe McDonald/Animals Animals; *r.* Dorey Sparre for SBG. 96: Hank Morgan/Rainbow. 97: *t.* Randall Hyman Photography; *b.* William Campbell/Peter Arnold. 106: *l.* James Craigmyle for SBG; *r.* James Craigmyle for SBG. 107: *t.* James Craigmyle for SBG; *b.* Bill Brooks/Masterfile Corporation. 108: *b.* C. Bowman/Picture Perfect USA. 110–111: *bkgd.* NASA. 112: *t.* © De Sazo/Photo Researchers, Inc.; *m.* © Carolyn Brown/Photo Researchers, Inc.; *b.l.* © Brian Brake/Photo Researchers, Inc.; *b.r.* Dennis Cox/ChinaStock. 114: *l.* Erich Lessing/Art Resource; *r.* The Bettmann Archive. 116: The Stock Market. 117: *t.* © B. Pougeoise/Explorer/Photo Researchers, Inc.; *b.* © Sabine Weiss/Rapho/Photo Researchers, Inc. 118: *t.* © Brian Yarvin/Photo Researchers, Inc.; *b.* Joe Viesti/Viesti Associates. 119: Joe Viesti/Viesti Associates. 121: *t.l.* Randall Hyman Photography; *t.r.* Martin Wendler/Peter Arnold; *b.* Randall Hyman Photography. 122: *t.* Randall Hyman Photography; *m.* Peter R. Hornby. 125: David Young Wolff/PhotoEdit. 126: *l.* Manfred Gottschalk/Tom Stack & Associates; *r.* Kunio Owaki/The Stock Market. 127: *t.* David Ball/The Stock Market; *b.* Rob Crandall/Rainbow. 128: © Bill Bachmann/Photo Researchers, Inc. 129: *t.* Comstock; *b.* © Farrell Grehan/Photo Researchers, Inc. 132–135: Tom Raymond/Fresh Air Photographics.

Illustrations Map Handbook: Stan Tusan, Alex Bloch/MKR Design. *Opposite* 1: Robert Roper. 4–9: Fiona Dunbar. 14–19: Bruce Armstrong. 20–24: Hugh Biber. 25–28: Andrew Shiff. 35: Fiona Dunbar. 36–37: Bob Brugger. 50–53: Olivia McElroy. 58–59: Tungwai Chau. 60–61: Jeffrey Chapman. 63–67: Margaret Cusack. 68–69: Gil Ashby. 71: Bob Brugger. 72: Alan Wallner. 72–73: Paul Meisel. 76–78: Randy Hamblin. 80–83: Kim Fernandes. 87: Byron Gin. 88–91: Tom Leonard. 92–95: Randy Chewning. 96: John Kastner. 102–103: David Clar. 105–108: Deborah Haley Melmon. 110–111: Sharon Vargo. 120: Don Madden. 120–124: Andrew Shiff. 125: Don Madden. 126–136: David Clar. 143–148: Andrew Shiff.